A BIRTHDAY
GIFT FROM
JUNE 2012

CELEBRATING
NEW ZEALAND
WINE

NH
NEW
HOLLAND

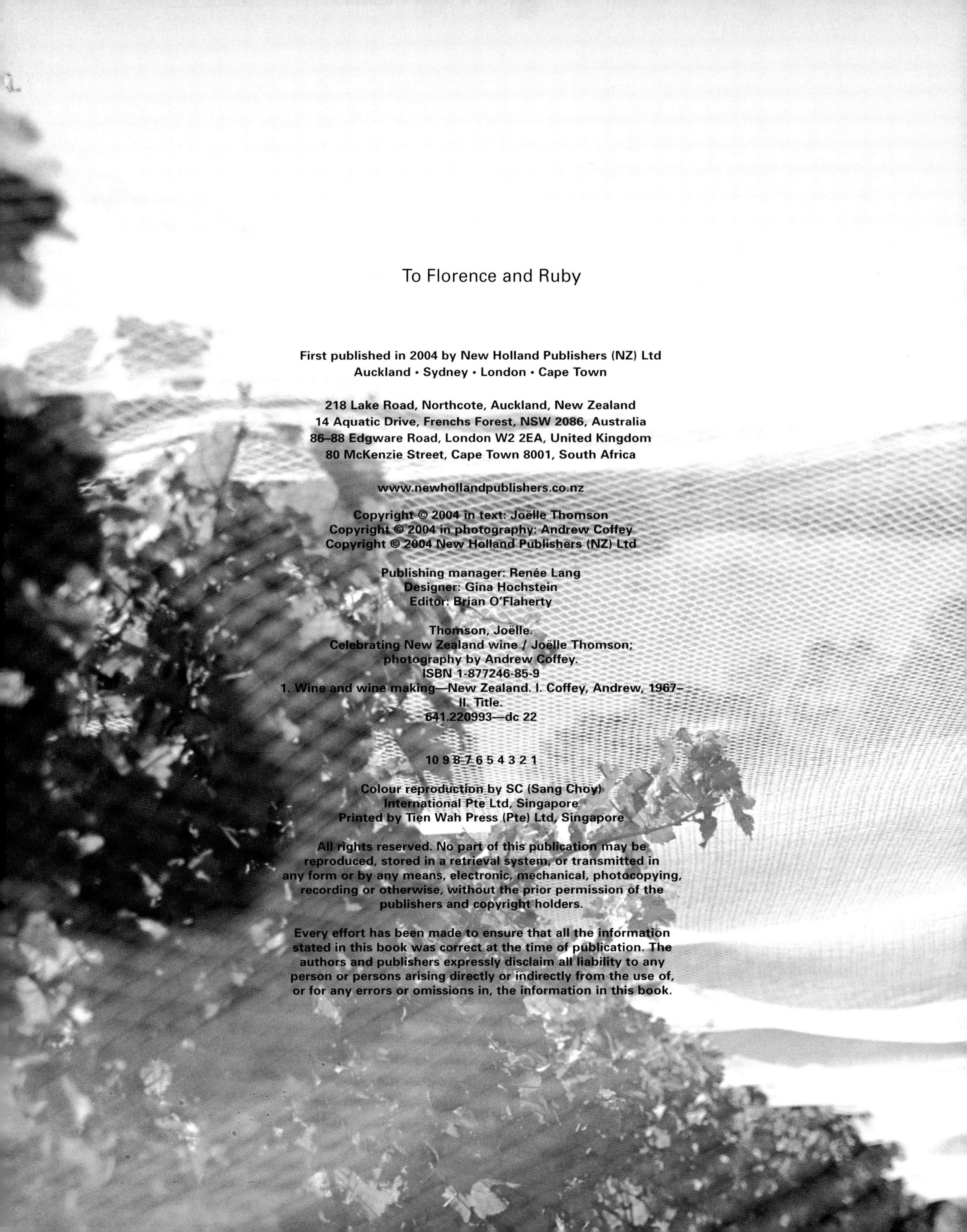

To Florence and Ruby

First published in 2004 by New Holland Publishers (NZ) Ltd
Auckland · Sydney · London · Cape Town

218 Lake Road, Northcote, Auckland, New Zealand
14 Aquatic Drive, Frenchs Forest, NSW 2086, Australia
86–88 Edgware Road, London W2 2EA, United Kingdom
80 McKenzie Street, Cape Town 8001, South Africa

www.newhollandpublishers.co.nz

Copyright © 2004 in text: Joëlle Thomson
Copyright © 2004 in photography: Andrew Coffey
Copyright © 2004 New Holland Publishers (NZ) Ltd

Publishing manager: Renée Lang
Designer: Gina Hochstein
Editor: Brian O'Flaherty

Thomson, Joëlle.
Celebrating New Zealand wine / Joëlle Thomson;
photography by Andrew Coffey.
ISBN 1-877246-85-9
1. Wine and wine making—New Zealand. I. Coffey, Andrew, 1967–
II. Title.
641.220993—dc 22

10 9 8 7 6 5 4 3 2 1

Colour reproduction by SC (Sang Choy)
International Pte Ltd, Singapore
Printed by Tien Wah Press (Pte) Ltd, Singapore

CELEBRATING
NEW ZEALAND
WINE

Joëlle Thomson

photography by Andrew Coffey

NEW
HOLLAND

Contents

Foreword

Celebrating New Zealand Wine is an elegant and artful celebration of New Zealand's remarkable emergence as a producer of world-class wines. It is about the people that made it happen and the land that always had the potential to make it happen.

In the world of wine New Zealand's rapid rise in the past 30 years is nothing short of sensational. Three decades ago our wines by today's standards were undrinkable and wine exports were non-existent. Wine drinkers were far more likely to choose a local port, sherry or carbonated sparkling wine than a table wine. Table wine was typically labelled as 'Claret', 'Chablis' or 'Burgundy' rather than the grape variety names that are now common currency.

Today our wines are sold at high prices in restaurants and wine stores throughout the world. Vineyards now carpet valleys where sheep once grazed; wineries boast some of the country's leading restaurants while overseas wine buyers include us on their shopping list. We serve and savour New Zealand wines with pride. We have become a wine nation.

Celebrating New Zealand Wine weaves history (did you know that Wairarapa's first wines were planted in 1883?) with fact (Marlborough's vineyard area doubled in the five years to 2004).

The tapestry is made even richer by the stories of many wine-makers. Their stories are full of candour ('We were novices, nobody knew anything about viticulture … but we gave it a go' – Alan Scott, Allan Scott Wines), bravado ('Who says Hawke's Bay can't make bloody good pinot' – John Hancock, Trinity Hill), modesty ('I find it extraordinary that our syrah gets so much acceptance' – Dr Neil McCallum, Dry River) and optimism ('If you want to make internationally competitive table wines with pinot noir, this is where you need to grow grapes…' – Jeff Sinnott, Amisfield).

Author Joëlle Thomson takes us on a journey through the country's wine regions, providing us with a big picture of each wine area before narrowing the focus to the people who have shaped some of its more famous wines. We learn that there are no instant recipes for success, just a lot of trial, error, hard work and sometimes a bit of luck.

Andrew Coffey's brilliant photography tells a story that at times so smoothly fits the text that his camera lens could easily have been the author's eye. Coffey captures both landscape and the people that shape it using powerful images that amplify Joëlle's writing. He gives us a macro view of hills and valleys before zooming in for a close-up of leaf or label. My favourite shot is ducks in a Nelson vineyard.

Celebrating New Zealand Wine is a good read, a visual feast and a valuable perspective on a diverse and complex wine industry. It provides a glimpse of where we've been and an indication of where we're heading.

The quality and scale of New Zealand's wine has grown rapidly but the industry faces new challenges from an aggressive and unforgiving global marketplace. When I turned the last page I felt pride in what has been achieved and confidence in our ability to go even further.

New Zealand wine is in good heart.

Bob Campbell, MW

Introduction

Every wine lover has an instant when a wine tastes so great that the desire to repeat the experience means life is never quite the same again. For me, that moment came in 1991 over a bottle of Kumeu River Sémillon, shared with a very close friend, at a top BYO restaurant in the unlikely, wind-blown suburb of Northland, in Wellington.

Like most wine drinkers, I was more interested in the taste of the wine in the bottle than the vintage on the label, so I haven't got a clue what year it was from but every sip saw my growing interest in wine become a full-blown passion. And although Kumeu River Wines no longer makes sémillon, I am not alone in having been profoundly influenced by wine because of theirs.

Halfway through writing this introduction, a friend who works in the New Zealand wine industry divulged that his own infatuation with wine began with a glass of San Marino Dry Red, way back before the San Marino winery changed names to become Kumeu River Wines.

There are few wineries as influential as this one anywhere on earth. Kumeu River's journey began when the late Mate Brajkovich and his parents, Mick and Baba Kate, bought land in Kumeu in 1944. Today, Mate's wife, Melba, and her three sons, Michael, Milan and Paul, work at the still small, quality oriented winery together.

Michael is the winemaker and was the first New Zealander to pass the Master of Wine examination in 1989. Four years earlier, he made a chardonnay that was disparaged by many in the country's wine community. Back then and right up until 1991, müller-thurgau was the most planted grape variety in the country, so it was no surprise that a chardonnay made in the mould of a good French white burgundy rather than a tutti-fruity Kiwi white went down like a lead balloon. But Brajkovich persevered and now both Kumeu River Chardonnay and Mate's Vineyard Chardonnay are among the best wines in this country every year.

Things have changed dramatically over the last two decades in other ways, too. Even in the mid-1990s, Central Otago was viewed with deep suspicion by many, and sauvignon blanc was the beginning, middle and end of New Zealand wine.

Today Central Otago is the country's fourth biggest wine region and while sauvignon blanc is the most planted grape variety in the country, many Kiwi winemakers are beginning to make merlots and pinot noirs that are commanding high price tags, winning medals and gaining rave reviews all over the world. Some winemakers are even turning out delicious gamay noir, montepulciano and viognier.

The number of grapevines planted in all of New Zealand's wine regions is growing and the importance of individual grape varieties is still changing as the New Zealand wine industry comes of age.

Celebrating New Zealand Wine is a snapshot of many of the developments along this journey, featuring its eight main wine regions, many of the vineyards and the people who toil in them today. The intention of this book is not to provide the latest production statistics, climate data or soil information. My own book shelves and those of many who will read this book are already happily groaning under the strain of impressive tomes devoted to these matters.

The people and vineyards featured in this book are representative rather than all-inclusive of this country's grape-growing and winemaking scene today. It has not been possible to feature all of the 460-plus wineries in New Zealand today, but photographer Andrew Coffey and I have chosen a diverse range of regions, wineries and faces that make up the industry. Most importantly, we have tried to convey some of the passion of this country's winemakers.

The idea that a country whose Maori name, Aotearoa, means 'Land of the Long White Cloud' could ever become a serious wine-producing nation seems paradoxical. But as winemakers everywhere love to tell, the greatest wines in the world come from the edgiest growing conditions.

And Aotearoa is definitely an edgy place in which to grow grapes and make wine. It has a tricky maritime climate and is isolated from the biggest wine markets in the world (in the northern hemisphere). None of these factors has dampened this country's wine scene or the enthusiam of its winemakers.

In the last decade, the nation's vineyard area has tripled, from just 6110 hectares in 1995 to a predicted 18,247 by 2005, with more massive growth expected for the rest of this decade.

The biggest challenge facing the local wine scene today is in coming to terms with being an industry that caters predominantly to the global market rather than being focused on the domestic one.

In 1993, total New Zealand wine exports were around NZ$48 million. By 2003 that figure grew to NZ$281 million and it continues to climb. This means that local winemakers and marketers need to spend more time in the new markets of Australia, New York and Washington as well as in the traditional United Kingdom one.

Like their Australian counterparts, New Zealand winemakers are frequent travellers, clocking up loads of air miles and vast storehouses of wine memories and plenty of experiences to put into practice – or avoid – back home. This helps New Zealand winemakers to gain an indepth understanding of the global wine market, its trends and consumers' evolving tastes.

And as their marketing aims change so too will the taste of their wines as they grow in stature and style to meet a wider range of consumers around the world.

New Zealand's wine scene has blossomed into a tricky to manage but beautiful looking teenager, full of promise. If we are able to convey the excitement and passion in this youthful and vibrant industry, then *Celebrating New Zealand Wine* will have more than achieved its purpose.

Before you begin reading this book, you really should have a glass of wine in your hand, raised to the New Zealand wine industry.

In a little over a century, a handful of fledgling wineries run by young, often inexperienced winemakers have evolved into one of the world's most dynamic modern wine scenes.

There is a lot to celebrate about the journey. This book toasts that coming of age.

Joëlle Thomson

Acknowledgements

It would have been impossible to write and photograph this book without the assistance of many wineries. Marlborough winemaker Allan Scott's contribution to our transport and accommodation was beyond the call of duty but his most lavish assistance was time. Over lengthy, humorous discussions, Scott candidly recollected planting the first grapes in Marlborough – not always successfully.

On that same trip, I tasted montepulciano grapes, which were so ripe, plump and red it was almost impossible to believe they were grown in that region at Hans and Therese Herzog's winery. The proof was before my eyes and the camera as we picked them off the vine and tasted their unbelievably sweet flavours. The meal at this Swiss couple's restaurant also proved to be a superlative experience.

Relatively late in the putting together of this book, wine fanatic John Buchanan spent time with photographer Andrew Coffey at the Seventeen Valley vineyard, just south of Blenheim township.

In Nelson, Tim and Judy Finn shared their favourite wines as well as a stunningly good cheese fondue on one of the region's typically sunny days.

In Waipara, North Canterbury, the hospitality of Buffy and Michael Eaton at Mountford Estate was unceasing. Even though this couple have stopped using their stylish country home as one of the greatest homestays in the country, they welcomed us, literally, with open arms for a couple of days' stay.

We appreciated the lasagne and fresh salad in the sun at Muddy Water Estate in Waipara. The food magically materialised just as our tummies started rumbling and as I was wondering where on earth we would find food in Waipara, and winemaker Belinda Gould brought out riesling and pinot noir from different vintages, made in a variety of styles and sealed various ways.

As essential to the book's completion as good wine was more than our share of decent coffee, like that served to us in the smoko room at Millton Estate one warm Saturday morning in Gisborne. It helped kickstart a busy day of recording winemaker James Millton's musings on making wine and photographing his and Annie's tiny but important Naboth's Vineyard.

And Chic Mackie at Glencarrigh Homestay in Gisborne provided not only deliciously comfortable accommodation but also fascinating insights into the history of Gisborne.

For the first three of our journeys to Hawke's Bay, the sun would not shine, but when the Bay finally turned on its usually reliable sunshine on other trips there, we repeatedly saw why this is the country's most versatile and varied wine region.

Although I could not be present, due to inclement weather, Andrew assures me that the winemakers' barbecue in Martinborough was a brilliant social event. And thanks to Richard Riddiford and Larry McKenna, both Andrew and I (when the clouds cleared) were able to get to Martinborough, which is such a chic little town. It is still pint-sized but, due to the region's wine scene, Martinborough has grown to bursting point with good cafés, wine bars and restaurants. It even has a truly excellent women's clothing store, but I digress...

In the Deep South, ice and snow grounded me in Central Otago for an extra day and a half of what had already been a fascinating trip through one of the most dramatic, spectacular, 'lost for words because it's so beautiful' places on the planet. Winemakers Jeff Sinnott and Grant Taylor are just two of the region's most passionate experimental producers and their time and knowledge were greatly appreciated. As were winemaker Matt Dicey's, during conversations in both Central and Auckland, during which he quietly confessed to an intense desire to make decent quantities of top-quality riesling. There are many others who shared time, meals and knowledge with us and far more who did not get the opportunity to do so.

Thank you to all of the winemakers in New Zealand today.

RIGHT: Today Corbans Viticulture, at Whenuapai in West Auckland, is one of the country's largest vine nurseries and grape grafters, as shown in these pictures of grafting. Joe Corban, aptly called the grandfather of New Zealand viticulture by many in the country's wine industry, began what is now Corbans Viticulture in the late 1980s. Like all members of the Corban family, wine and grapes were in his blood, and when the wine business left family ownership, Joe began work with what he knew best – grapes.

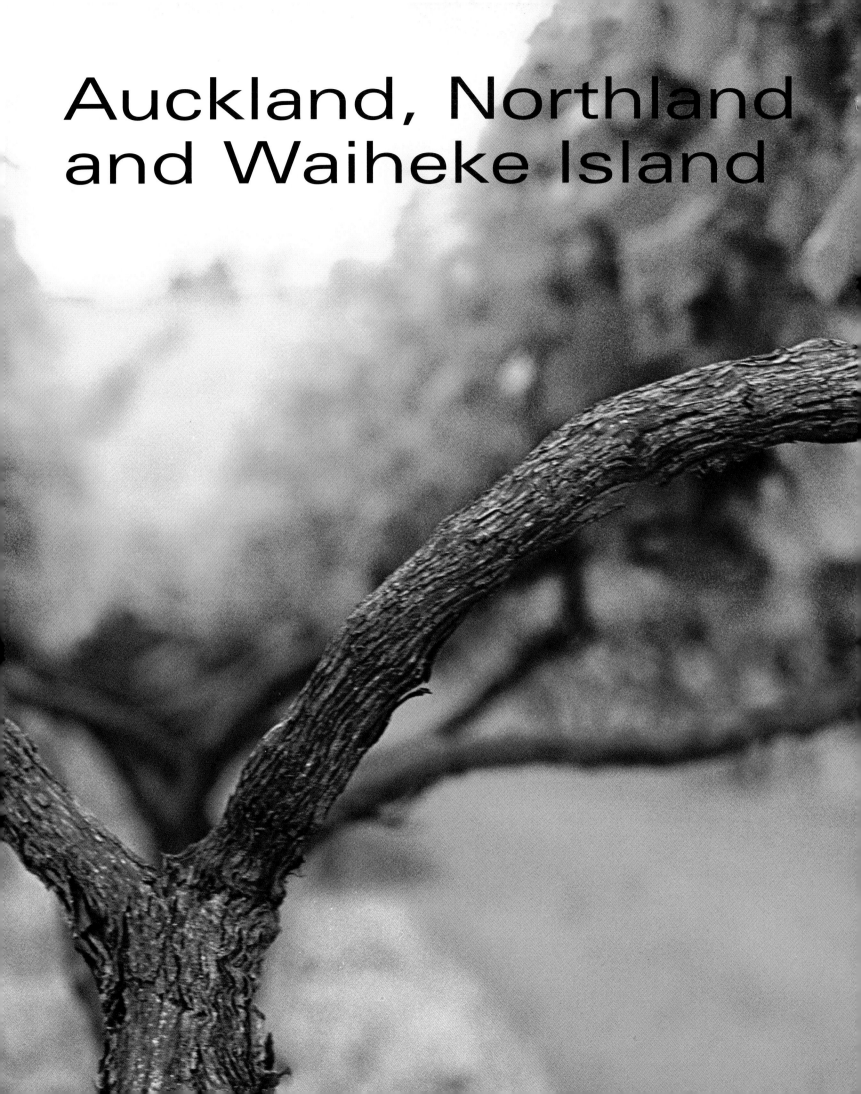

Auckland, Northland
and Waiheke Island

The string bean of land that stretches from Northland south to Auckland and its seaside cousin, Waiheke Island, is home to a diverse range of vineyards and wineries, each facing climatic challenges that would cause many winemakers to throw in their wine-stained towels…

Picture the scene: grape-growers, winemakers and family members stride casually down Henderson's main street, shotguns slung over their shoulders, and wander into a store for provisions before heading back to the vineyard to fire a few more rounds at the birds trying to get at their grapes. As unlikely as it seems this scene typified life for many West Auckland winemakers less than a century ago. Not only has the New Zealand culture dramatically changed but urban sprawl, industrial development and ever-growing motorways have swallowed vast tracts of vineyard land. It's not as if the wine industry has thrown up great protests, either, with many Auckland winemaking families still thriving but buying in grapes from Gisborne, Hawke's Bay and Marlborough.

Nearly two centuries ago, in 1819, New Zealand's first grapes were planted by missionary Samuel Marsden in Northland.

And while the regions of Auckland and Northland are the backbone of the New Zealand wine industry, they are responsible for a mere trickle of the country's total wine output.

Auckland is still the most important wine region in New Zealand because it is the base of the country's wine industry. It is here, more than any other region, that winemakers determine the styles of wine that the country will produce in high volumes.

Today the city is home to the headquarters of New Zealand's three largest wineries and numerous small winemakers, who work doggedly to retain their land, identity and winemaking heritage.

The late winemaker Lionel Collard is typical of the Auckland wine fraternity. Dragged out of the army halfway through the Second World War to help on his family's fruit orchard, he established a winery that grew to become one of the country's largest.

'When my father and mother became ill, in 1942, they sent me home to run the place, which annoyed me no end because I had just got a very good job as a junior staff officer,' recalled Collard.

It was a privilege speaking with this incredibly lucid man, whose passion for the New Zealand wine industry is characterised by dogged determination, belied by his softly spoken temperament.

PREVIOUS PAGES: Lyre trellising at Mate's Vineyard, Kumeu River Wines, West Auckland.
ABOVE: Vintage comes first in the north of the North Island.
RIGHT: Planting new vines in West Auckland at Kumeu River Wines, which is widely regarded as one of New Zealand's best wineries.

After working on the family orchard for a few years, Collard's uncles, the Averill brothers, decided that wine was more promising. Like most in the early New Zealand wine industry, Collard built a name for his winery in the mid-twentieth century with wines made from hybrids and crosses prior to using classic grape varieties. His sons now run the business, and the winery buys in most of their grapes from Marlborough and Hawke's Bay. They retain a five-hectare vineyard in Auckland.

The region can be a tricky one in which to grow grapes to turn into high-quality wine but ironically Auckland's best wines come from grapes grown solely in the area, at Kumeu River Wines.

Disparate geography is one of the defining features of the vast Auckland wine region, which encompasses several sub-regions. The region begins in the north at Matakana and Mahurangi, both of which are situated inland from the quaint east coast town of Warkworth, about an hour's drive north of Auckland city.

The most historic area is Henderson in West Auckland. Further west are Kumeu, Huapai and Waimauku, in the take-me-by-surprise green countryside situated around the small industrial township of Kumeu, which many would like to see gentrified in order to stimulate the strong wine tourism potential.

Waiheke Island is part of the Auckland wine region too. Like most Auckland wineries, many on this island buy in grapes from Marlborough and Hawke's Bay as well as growing their own.

The smallest of all the wine-producing sub-regions is South Auckland, comprised of a cluster of small vineyards and wineries in Clevedon. Once principally home to dairy and pastoral farms, the area now has horticultural, floricultural and equestrian businesses, along with winemaking. New vineyards here are being developed by Villa Maria Wines near Auckland International Airport.

Viticultural growth in the entire region is partly accounted for by the smattering of small new wineries in and around Matakana and the tiny vineyards south of the city around Clevedon.

Montana Wines has its HQ in east Auckland, which is not a grape-growing area but a large quantity of wine is made here, thanks to grapes that find their way to Auckland from the company's vineyards in other regions.

Land of the long white cloud is the translation of Aotearoa, the Maori name for New Zealand, originally applied to the North Island. It sums up perfectly the biggest challenges that the country's maritime climate presents for winemakers all over New Zealand, most pertinently in Auckland and Northland.

There is a dramatic increase in rainfall and humidity the further north grapes are planted and that, coupled with highly fertile soils, make this region far from ideal for a wine industry.

Add to that a Victorian settler culture with a penchant for binge beer drinking and its attendant prohibitionists at the turn of the twentieth century and you have a recipe for anything but a thriving wine scene. Despite all of these early stumbling blocks, European settlers in the late nineteenth and early twentieth centuries laid the foundations for the headquarters of what is now one of the world's most dynamic wine industries. Assid Abraham Corban, Joseph Babich, Mate Brajkovich and a host of others, mainly Europeans, not only planted grapes, built wineries and made a vinous cocktail of wine styles in a beer-obsessed land, they imbued their families with the same heady dose of drive, passion and tenacity that they possessed.

These families' descendants are based in and around the Auckland region, and some of the region's wineries today are small in size but huge in historical significance.

In 2002, the area held 448 hectares of vines, with predictions that this would grow to 519 hectares by 2004 – a 16 percent increase. Despite which, by 2005 these three regions will still be home to only about three percent of New Zealand's vineyards, according to the *New Zealand Wine and Grape Industry Statistical Annual*.

Chardonnay reigns supreme in Auckland and Northland. It suits the regions well because it is a relatively early ripening grape variety, meaning it can avoid problematic late summer rain.

Kumeu River winemaker Michael Brajkovich agrees with the notion that relatively early ripening grape varieties are best suited to the Auckland climate. Chardonnay has pride of place in the vineyards and winery that he and his family own and operate at Kumeu, West Auckland. The business was established by his father, the late Mate Brajkovich, and is now operated by Mate's wife, Melba, and her three sons – Michael, Paul and Milan.

'In Auckland, on the vine chardonnay matures early enough to ensure that it is always ripe enough to make quality wine from, but later season varieties can be difficult in cool years,' says Brajkovich, citing cabernet sauvignon as a grape that is not suited to Auckland's growing conditions.

LEFT: Merlot is the most promising red grape at the aptly named West Brook Winery, in West Auckland.
BELOW: The late Lionel Collard, whose winery is on the now busy Lincoln Road, remembered a time when the street was covered in red grape juice, as freshly harvested grapes were trucked to the local wineries.

Kumeu River Wines accounts for a small quantity of wine with a total emphasis on quality. Unlike other wineries in the region Kumeu River Wines grows all of its grapes in Auckland, under the fastidious care of Milan Brajkovich, the viticulturist of the family.

As far as growth goes, Michael Brajkovich says most of theirs has been the revision of grape varieties already planted to more suitable ones.

'We have been busy replanting better clones of some of the grapes we already had and putting in both new rootstocks and new clones. We have pulled out a merlot vineyard and all of our sauvignon blanc and in their place we are putting chardonnay, pinot noir and pinot gris.'

'The problems here are mainly about humidity and heat but you are also looking at land prices being quite high. The fact that we're here already has a big bearing on why we stay and we have the land and the rigorous practices in our vineyards all set in place to make top quality wine.'

The viticultural practices Brajkovich speaks of include a strong focus on reducing the amount of chemicals used in the vineyard. Despite the fact that vigorous leaf-plucking might seem a logical answer to reducing rot and mildew problems, Brajkovich says it is not so simple.

Northland, Auckland and Waiheke Island have a high profile when it comes to wine-making but they are responsible for only about three percent of the total New Zealand grape-growing area.

'We don't want to expose the bunches too much so it's a matter of achieving balance rather than leaf-plucking for the sake of it.'

Brajkovich was 12 years old when he knew he wanted to work with wine. For him, the wine industry is family, and he took over the winemaking reins from his late father, Mate.

As far as red wine goes, Brajkovich has high hopes for pinot noir but says there is a lot of work to get this grape to the stage that it is ready to produce top quality wines from the Auckland region.

'I am confident that in a few years' time we will be able to say that pinot noir is Auckland's best red variety.'

As to whether the winery will remain in the family, Brajkovich says that is the family's ideal. And there are plenty of third generation members to make the ideal possible.

LEFT: Vines are not only pruned vigorously at Kumeu River Wine's Mate's Vineyard in West Auckland but the prunings are then burnt to lower the risk of any possible disease spread in the vineyard.
ABOVE: Vine prunings at Mate's Vineyard.

BELOW: A vine at Coopers Creek in West Auckland, among the biggest wineries in the region today but, like many, one which sources most of its grapes from Hawke's Bay and Marlborough. RIGHT: Mate's Vineyard spills down the hill from winemaker Michael Brajkovich's home in Kumeu. It and the chardonnay from the vineyard are named after Mate Brajkovich, Michael's father and the winery's founder.

'For us, wine is not just a brand that can be exploited or changed. It's a long term thing that we work with and we are part of its evolution. We make decisions for the long term, not for just the next two or three years.'

The most planted grapes, after chardonnay, are merlot, cabernet sauvignon, cabernet franc, pinot noir and pinotage.

'Auckland will always be great for merlot,' says Tony Soljan, of the distinctive new Soljans winery, on State Highway 2 in Kumeu.

Like most of the region's winemakers, the majority of his grapes come from Marlborough, Hawke's Bay and Gisborne but he keeps an area of vines planted in the region. The strongest performers of these he says are chardonnay, merlot and pinotage.

'All grapes grown in Auckland today produce better flavours than they used to, due to new virus-free clones that provide us with more fruit flavours and better all-round wines.'

Auckland is also home to small amounts of gewürztraminer, syrah, malbec, sauvignon blanc, pinot gris, palomino, breidecker, chasselas, chenin blanc, müller-thurgau, sémillon, sylvaner and blauberger. And there are also tiny quantities of 'other red varieties', like chambourcin.

A fan of pinotage grown in Auckland is Peter Babich, who enjoys having an attractive barrier of mainly pinotage grapevines growing between the Babich winery and its nearest neighbours: a fast-growing suburb on what was once just bare Henderson hillside.

But Peter Babich is cynical about Auckland's grape quality. 'We'd go broke if we only relied on grapes grown in Henderson,' he says, with a laugh.

Like other members of his family-owned winery, Babich is highly appreciative of local city councillors today who encourage the Babich family to preserve some of their original vineyards. This ensures that a slice of local and family history is kept intact and it preserves their historic winery's connection with the land their forebears planted.

Until the 1930s the entire West Auckland area was known, in jest, as the 'Wild West'.

Third-generation grape-grower Joe Corban well remembers walking into Henderson with a gun over his shoulder, in the 1930s.

'Anyone behaving like that now would be arrested but back then it was just the way we got around. I used that gun to keep birds away from the vines so I had it on me all the time,' says Corban. 'We were just going about daily duties without any hint of a threat to anybody.'

The most threatening thing members of some of these early wine families did inadvertently affected themselves.

'It was nothing,' says Corban, 'for a whole generation of family members to be spraying chemicals that we now know are lethal to human health and well-being. In the 1920s and 1930s these toxins were seen as magic potions in the vineyards and they were liberally applied without wearing either gloves or masks.'

The climate in the Auckland region has always presented big challenges to winemakers, says Corban, who recalls his grandfather's vineyard as being on 'less than suitable soil types'.

'There was a constant battle against mildew because of the humidity and rain. Strong chemicals seemed like the solution, but we didn't realise how bad they could be to human health.'

There are other ways to combat these viticultural challenges and winemakers who persist with growing their own grapes in the region spend lots of time in their vineyards to nip problems in the bud.

'I would never bag Auckland as a wine region but it is easier to find a better microclimate in Hawke's Bay or Marlborough in which to grow grapes,' says David Babich.

Less than five percent of the grapes used by the Babich family today are grown at the now-diminished family vineyard on Babich Road, Henderson, which is the headquarters of this relatively large New Zealand winery.

For Babich, Marlborough sauvignon forms the largest part of their production and grapes from Hawke's Bay's make their big-ticket wines, like Irongate Chardonnay and Irongate Cabernet Sauvignon.

'Even at a young age I could see wine was an interesting industry with the potential for a great lifestyle, the chance to meet lots of interesting people, travel and work for yourself. Who wouldn't want to work in an industry like that?' Michael Brajkovich, Kumeu River Wines

One of the greenest, lushest corners of West Auckland is Waimauku, where the large Matua Valley Winery is based, and also winemaker Anthony and Sue Ivicevich's new West Brook Winery.

Anthony speaks with admiration about his grandfather and uncle, who started Panorama Vineyard in Henderson in the 1930s.

'When housing started to move in all round the old winery, we realised that it had ceased to become an attractive destination for people to come to,' says Ivicevich, adding that the local council was more focused on housing than wineries.

'It was understandable. We only had seven acres and it just seemed like it was a matter of time before we were forced to go.' In the early 2000s, the Ivicevich family shifted of their own volition, moving slightly further west, and planting a small new vineyard around the winery.

West Brook Winery sources most of its grapes from Marlborough, Gisborne and Hawke's Bay.

'Long term, we would like to put some of our own vineyards in but for now it's working best to make wine from grapes we buy.'

Ivicevich describes the climate at Waimauku as slightly cooler than in Auckland city and says he also experiences between seven to 10 percent less rain than the city.

'Our soils are light, friable, free-draining clays with good water run-off. We think we can have a whack at pinot noir and probably make a really good one.'

Montana, Villa Maria and Nobilo are the country's three largest wine companies, all founded by European immigrants who made wine mainly in order to have some to drink. Once others became passionate about and involved in the growing wine scene, the output of these producers increased steadily throughout the twentieth century, resulting in take-overs and buy-outs and eventually even the largest were taken over.

Montana Wines is New Zealand's largest wine producer. The company passed out of family hands in gradual stages from the early 1970s to the early 1980s. As well as being a winemaker, Montana Wines is now also a wine distributor, importer and part of the large global drinks corporate, Allied Domecq.

Montana Wines began when Dalmatian immigrant Ivan Yukich planted his first vines in the Waitakere Ranges, which flank Henderson in West Auckland, in 1944. His sons Frank and Mate led the winery's expansion into Marlborough, in 1973, revolutionising the New Zealand wine industry, setting its profile on an ever-increasing international trajectory.

ABOVE: Vines on their way to being planted at Kumeu River Wines.
TOP RIGHT: David Babich, assistant GM at the medium-sized New Zealand winery, Babich Wines, on Babich Road, West Auckland.
TOP FAR RIGHT: Kumeu River's trellising technique effectively keeps fungal diseases at bay in a region where humidity is one of the greatest challenges to winemakers.
BELOW RIGHT: Vines at Matua Valley Winery are mainly planted for show, in the picturesque Waimauku Valley.

BELOW: Netting being laid out at Coopers Creek Vineyard on State Highway 16, Huapai, West Auckland. The winery was founded by accountant Andrew Hendry and winemaker Randy Weaver and is now owned by Hendry and his wife, Cyndy.
RIGHT: Rob Scott, quality assurance technician at Montana Wines in Glen Innes, Auckland.
FAR RIGHT: Bottles awaiting labelling at Montana Wines.

In 1973, Montana Wines sold a 40 percent shareholding to Seagram. The relationship between the brothers and the shareholder was turbulent and Montana passed into corporate hands completely when Lion Breweries took over in 1982.

In 2000, Montana Wines acquired what was then the second largest New Zealand wine company, Corbans Wines.

Corbans Wines began when Assid Abraham Corban emigrated from Lebanon to New Zealand in 1892 and planted his first vines in Henderson, in 1902. His wife Najibie and their first children joined him in 1896.

Corbans Wines grew to become one of the biggest wineries in the country, initially making large quantities of fortified wines and later moving into table wine production.

In the 1970s it was swallowed up by Rothmans. The Corban brand name has remained strong ever since, despite other buy-outs. Even with its biggest rival now at the helm, many Corbans-branded wines are among the best value of their type in the country. Members of the family now own Ngatarawa Wines in Hawke's Bay and Corbans Viticulture in West Auckland and are involved actively at many levels of the New Zealand wine industry, not least because their legacy continues in ways that many modern winemakers are not even aware of. Members of the Corban family have been hugely instrumental in New Zealand in the pioneering of stainless steel tank fermentation, bench-grafting and other innovative wine technology.

The Nobilo Wine Group is now the second biggest winery in New Zealand and is owned by the Australian-based Hardy Wine Company, owned by the world's largest wine company, Constellation Brands.

Nobilo Wines grew from an already sizeable winery to a large one when, in 1998, it purchased Selak's Wines.

In New Zealand Nobilo Wines is best known for its plethora of interesting wine styles and accessibly priced brands. Despite this reputation, chief executive officer Brian Vieceli says the company is not trying to be all things to all people.

'We're aware that we don't have a great deal of super-premium wines in the range and now that we have gone through this massive expansion phase, we can focus on growing the top end wines.'

Of the big three, Villa Maria is the only truly New Zealand winery, in that it is privately owned by a New Zealander.

Chairman George Fistonich started out as winemaker when he took over the reins of his father's small winery in his early twenties. He started by selling wine at the gate then became a sales manager in 1968 and, from 1970 onwards, Fistonich says he doubled the sales every year.

Since then, Villa Maria Wines has grown to become a group of wineries, incorporating the Auckland headquarters and the Hawke's Bay-based Esk Valley Wines and Vidals Wines. Although most of Villa Maria's grapes are grown in Hawke's Bay and Marlborough, a new vineyard and winery headquarters is being established on a 40-hectare site inside an extinct volcano, Waitemokia, in South Auckland, not far from Auckland International Airport.

The entranceway to George Fistonich's new Villa Maria winery, headquarters, conference facility, vineyard and, soon to be café and restaurant, is a dramatic descent into the crater in one of Auckland's prettiest industrial corners. The exit to the winery will be a gentle drive up a steep bank, after which drivers will be rewarded with an almost 360-degree vista of Manukau Harbour, horses ambling along a grassy bank and then a clear view to the heads of the harbour on the not too distant horizon.

Fistonich has even more long term plans for this unlikely out of the way setting, which include the eventual construction of plush self-contained accommodation, tennis courts and walkways and possibly even a golf course.

Grapevines were planted extensively in this area, until airport authorities insisted in the late 1980s and early 1990s that they be pulled out. The land was said to be needed for runways that never eventuated. Shareholders and others who grew grapes for Villa Maria Wines pulled out all their vines. Fistonich remembers with passion the high quality and, in his words, delicious taste, of gewürztraminer made from grapes grown in the area and says he looks forward to producing even better flavours from the new vineyard.

'All of the grapes we're planting there are to be early ripeners, like gewürztraminer, chardonnay, pinot noir, merlot and possibly some pinot gris,' he says, adding that this way the climatic challenges will be easier to overcome.

'I'm not so interested in being the third biggest winery in the country as long as we are first in quality,' says the quietly spoken Fistonich.

The new winery will produce more wine but Fistonich insists he does not want to compete with large global wine corporates: 'You have got to be big enough to survive in an increasingly competitive climate but we don't want to put out lots of cheap wine for the sake of survival.'

Matakana and neighbouring Mahurangi account for less than one percent of the country's annual vineyard. In 2003 there were around 80 hectares of vines planted in this sub-region, with most of the wineries being tiny operations; expansion is unlikely to dramatically increase the area planted.

The families who formed the backbone of the New Zealand wine industry today have spawned new enterprises at Matakana, like Darryl Soljan's Ascension Vineyards.

'I chose Matakana because viticulturist Joe Corban once inspired me with his thoughts on the region's strong viticultural potential.'

Like most of the other wineries in Matakana and Mahurangi, food is an intrinsic part of the winery experience at Ascension.

Eighty percent of Soljan's wine production is made from locally planted grapes. Chardonnay, pinot gris, viognier, cabernet sauvignon, malbec, merlot and pinotage are planted locally and he buys in small quantities of riesling and pinot from Marlborough. The riesling grapes go towards making a medium to dry style of wine, while the pinot noir makes a vintage bubbly.

'The only reason we use grapes from Marlborough is that we love riesling and needed to have a wine to sell that was not bone-dry. You could grow riesling but the conditions are probably less than ideal for this grape.'

The private ownership of Villa Maria Wines flies in the face of the increasing globalisation of ownership in the wine world.

'We looked at climate data and soil information and decided we wanted to make small volumes of individual, single vineyard wines rather than big quantities of anything. This caters to our growing tourism market here, just north of Auckland city, but close enough to be very accessible to visitors.'

Soljan says in good years his cabernet sauvignon predominant red wine is good but it is only about one year in three that cabernet sauvignon grapes become fully ripe. 'This makes it pretty expensive to make and hard work.'

The biggest viticultural challenge in this part of the Auckland region, says Soljan, is combatting the humidity and rain.

'In order to work with these difficult elements, we focus on growing loose bunches of grapes and having early ripening varieties. Pinotage performs well and it sells its socks off at the winery with its nice soft gamey flavours.'

ABOVE: George Fistonich, one of New Zealand's most innovative winemakers-turned-chief executives, in the crater of an old volcano – the home of the new headquarters of his winery, Villa Maria. RIGHT: Matakana is an hour's drive north of Auckland city and slightly warmer and wetter in climate, but still part of this sprawling wine region.

Over the hill and about 10 minutes' drive away from Matakana is the Mahurangi Estate winery, built to a breathtakingly simple design, poised on top of a hill with a panoramic view. A relatively big winery for the sub-region, it is run by Hamish McDonald and owned by his family and a syndicate of about 200 others.

The impressively plain plywood and pine building looks north, capturing almost all-day sun and overlooking the vineyard.

Mahurangi Estate, Ransom and Brick Bay wineries are on the Mahurangi side of the region, while Ascension, Heron's Flight, Hyperion, Matakana Estate and Providence are on the Matakana side. They are often, inaccurately, lumped together and McDonald is keen to dispel the myth that their growing conditions are the same. The area is typical of the diversity that characterises the small wineries and their vineyards in and around the greater Auckland region.

Cabernet sauvignon, malbec, merlot and syrah rule the red roost in this region while chardonnay is the most widely planted white. Like almost everywhere else in New Zealand, viognier is tipped to be a hot prospect. McDonald sagely says he is keen to try it but only time will tell whether viognier from here turns out to be any good.

Traditional Italian red grape varieties are also being planted and made into wine at the well-established Heron's Flight winery in Matakana. Winemakers David Hoskins and Mary Evans produce a good sangiovese, having shied away from their focus on traditional French grape varieties.

'The climate in the region is going through a change in cycle, which is the reason for the change in focus on grape varieties,' says David Hoskins.

There is no doubt, however, that of all the varied red grapes Hoskins has grown, all have produced good quality wines since the winery began in 1991.

As to the question of using grapes grown in other regions to boost the production at Mahurangi Wines, McDonald is cagey.

'Philosophically we don't really want to blend inter-regionally but the determining factor will be the wine quality. If I can make a better wine because of that I will do it,' he explains. 'But it's not a plan because there are huge differences between grapes grown at Gimblett Road and Matakana and they might be irreconcilable when it comes to making wine.'

With a record of nearly nine inches of rain in one day, Mahurangi is a challenging place in which to grow grapes, says McDonald. What will make the area work – as much as the promising pinot gris and fast-growing cache of cabernet sauvignons – is the café scene.

'No one is ever going to plant grapes in this region in any sort of huge supply because of the vagaries of the climate, so having a café is a way of improving your margins and attracting visitors to enjoy the natural beauty of the place with a glass of local wine in their hand.'

A group of several winemakers in Matakana and Mahurangi is now working together to establish a regional identity to market the area and its wines.

Northland became the historic home of New Zealand wine when the country's first grapevines were planted there by missionary Samuel Marsden, in 1819.

Just over a decade later, in the 1830s, James Busby made the first wine ever produced in the country from a small vineyard near his home at Waitangi.

New Zealand's first commercial-scale winemaking operation was established in Northland in 1863, when Englishman Charles Levet planted his vineyard near to Kaipara Harbour and for decades he made a living from the wines he produced there.

'We're not just aiming at the top five percent of people who are interested only in wine. We want people to have the whole experience of visiting the region, tasting the wines and enjoying them with food rather than feeling the pressure to analyse them in a stark tasting-room environment.' Darryl Soljan, Ascension Vineyard

Today Northland is characterised by small wineries, sparsely spread and making a wide range of different wine styles, mainly from *Vitis vinifera* grapes and with the legacy of some of the hybrids and crosses that characterised the early New Zealand wine industry.

At first glance, the far north town of Kaitaia seems an extremely unlikely place in which to grow grapes, but for Monty Knight it is only natural that he should be utilising land here to make wine.

Knight's Okahu Estate vineyard began life as a two-hectare hobby and was for a long time the country's most northern winery, but the new Carrington Estate now takes that place.

In 2003, Knight was developing another 2.4 hectares of Kaitaia vineyards with other investors. This will increase his wine production

LEFT: The Nobilo winery in West Auckland is home to one of the largest tank farms in the country – this is one of New Zealand's top four large wineries.
ABOVE: A rare breed: a fifth-generation New Zealand winemaker, Darryl Soljan, at the small Ascension Vineyard in Matakana.

substantially when this vineyard starts yielding grapes in the middle of the decade. He also buys in grapes from Te Kauwhata, Gisborne and Hawke's Bay to meet demand for his wine, which has increased steadily over the last five years.

'I started the winery because I wanted to make a bit for myself as a hobby but you soon find out you can't really do it like that.'

Knight initially made the wine himself but now hires a full-time winemaker. His winery and vineyard are out on a limb.

The vineyard is in the middle of what he describes as 'a bit of a weird weather pattern', which actually shelters him from rain. He has pinpointed three areas in the far north that he describes as suitable for growing grapes because of their unique, sheltered microclimates, including his own land – a relatively flat area devoid of hills. 'Just 15 minutes away it's really hilly and also really rainy.'

Good fortune put him in the right place. 'I didn't start the vineyard because I was in the right place. I started it because I just happened to live here and have some land. It's lucky it also happens that this is a good place to grow grapes.'

Shiraz is Knight's most successful and widely produced wine from his local vineyard.

'Loose-bunched red grapes like shiraz, merlot, pinotage and cabernet franc really suit this climate because of the relatively high

'I just can't wait to get a decent vintage again. We do battle weather problems up here and because we don't make big quantities of wine anyway, when it gets tricky we just make even smaller amounts than usual.' Barbara Vuletich, Longview Estate

humidity, and we are also growing a thing called chambourcin, which can make a soft, cheerful, everyday drinking red wine.'

As far as white grapes go, Knight has pulled everything up bar chardonnay and he plans to experiment with viognier and verdelho.

Other small wineries in and around Kerikeri include Cottle Hill, Marsden Estate and Omata Estate, which is also a luxury lodge.

Martin and Kay van Lubeck manage Omata Estate's vineyard, restaurant and Omata Retreat in Russell. Owners David and Anne Gaze planted 10 acres of grapevines in the late 1990s and established the restaurant and lodge at the same time.

Chardonnay is predominant with syrah and merlot also planted.

'Syrah seems to be the thing doing the best at the moment,' says Kay van Lubeck.

ABOVE: Rod MacIvor, owner of the Marsden Estate in Kerikeri, in the far north.
RIGHT: Like all wineries in Northland, Omata Estate is home to a small number of wines.

The wine is made by Rod MacIvor at Marsden Estate and their vineyard manager, Gary Janson, is training to become a viticulturist.

'The general consensus up here is that syrah is the best and most promising red grape right now.'

At Marsden Estate, winemakers Rod and Cindy MacIvor grow the white grapes chardonnay and pinot gris and reds merlot, malbec, cabernet sauvignon, chambourcin and pinotage.

All of these wineries sell a steady stream of locally made wines via their own cafés and cellar doors.

South of this cluster of northern wineries is the region's oldest winery, Longview Estate, situated on State Highway 1 just outside Whangarei. Until the mid-1990s it was called Continental Wines.

Longview's owner and winemaker Mario Vuletich's aim is to make a top quality red wine. His best red has been the merlot-based Mario's Merlot, followed by Scarecrow Cabernet Sauvignon. But syrah is looking increasingly promising says Vuletich's wife, Barbara, who runs the business.

The couple were also growing pinot noir, which they pulled out in 2002 because, in Barbara's words, it just did not like the region.

Their most planted reds now are cabernet sauvignon, merlot, malbec and syrah. But recent vintages have been problematic here, as in many of New Zealand's other wine regions.

Longview Estate whites include barrique-fermented chardonnay, very small amounts of gewürztraminer and their most popular white wine of all, White Diamond.

This unusual white sells with incredible ease, despite the fact that it is not widely publicised and is made from the little-known hybrid grape called Niagara.

This grape is an American hybrid of concord and cassady grapes, created in New York in 1872.

Even today it is, according to Jancis Robinson's *Guide to Wine Grapes*, the most successful native white grape variety in New York State. It is also the most widely grown grape in Brazil, so its success here in New Zealand is hardly out of the blue.

'In recent years the success of White Diamond has even grown beyond our expectations,' explains Barbara.

'It is a very easy wine to drink with hot food because of its light style and medium sweetness, and it is good with Asian food.'

BELOW: Okahu Estate winemaker Jennifer Bound with winery owner and founder, Monty Knight.
RIGHT: The view back to Auckland City from Waiheke Island's Te Whau Vineyard.

All of the wines made at Longview Estate are sold via the very picturesque cellar door and distributed locally to restaurants with a small mail order service to those who are on the list.

As Vuletich says, with a bit of a laugh, 'We basically live off the huge number of tourists travelling on State Highway 1.'

Waiheke Island, a short ferry ride from Auckland, once considered an alternative lifestyler's paradise, is as mainstream as any Auckland surburb and one of the fastest growing residential areas in the region.

In terms of wine production, Waiheke is still a toddler in many ways. Although wine is first thought to have been made there in the 1950s by the Gradiska family, it took another three decades until the Goldwater family, now Waiheke Island's largest wine producers, began planting their first vineyard in 1978.

Every weekend Kim and Jeanette Goldwater and their children sailed to the island, where they planted grapevines and native trees and then returned to the city, exhuasted but stimulated, says daughter Gretchen Goldwater, who now helps run the winery.

Since then Waiheke Island has been planted widely with small vineyards, like Stephen White's Stonyridge Wines, arguably the best known Waiheke Island winery but ironically one of the smallest.

At the island's well-established Stonyridge, Stephen White is constantly tweaking a syrah-based red, which includes mourvedre, grenache and viognier. The white grape viognier has been included in this blend for only the last two years and is largely about tradition, says White. His rationale is about matching local wines to the traditional way they are made, in terms of grape varieties, in their homes. About nine years ago he began making Stonyridge Row 10 chardonnay, which is solely for the restaurant trade and mail order. He also now owns a property called Vina Del Mar on the northern slopes at Onetangi, from which he makes a Bordeaux blended red.

The turn of the millennium saw the establishment of Cable Bay Winery and Te Whau, both ambitious new ventures.

It's easy to love the wines from Cable Bay, which is owned by Neill and Denise Culley and destined to become one of the largest Waiheke Island producers.

Like many Waiheke winemakers, the Culleys are sourcing grapes from Marlborough to make high quality sauvignon blanc, with an emphasis on ripe flavours.

They are also fixated on red varieties, grown on the island, like merlot, malbec and cabernet sauvignon.

Tony Forsyth fell for Waiheke in the early 1980s after a trip out to the island to see if it really was the great getaway from Auckland city many of his friends declared it to be.

Back then it took over an hour by ferry to reach Waiheke and, with only two broken down buses on the island, getting around once there was slightly challenging.

'It was quite different in every respect to how it is today and there were only the Goldwaters here at that stage with Goldwater Estate, and Stephen White had just started establishing Stonyridge.

'I loved wine but I thought the Goldwaters were mad trying to make it on Waiheke,' says Tony Forsyth, who owns one of the newest vineyards and wineries on the island today, Te Whau.

In 1993, Tony and Moira Forsyth bought 28 acres of land and it took them the next seven years to give up their lives in the city and move to the island permanently. They have the steepest north-south planted vineyard in New Zealand on a 22-degree slope.

Chardonnay is planted at the vineyard's lowest point and merlot, cabernet sauvignon, malbec and cabernet franc jostle for space on the rest of the tiny site.

'The joy of the vineyard is its topography. It looks like it could be a windswept hole but mercifully it's relatively sheltered. The wind goes over the top of it.'

With annual production of just 500 to 700 cases, Te Whau is one of New Zealand's smallest wineries. Its survival depends not just on the wine but also on its restaurant.

At Goldwater Estate, the emphasis is changing towards merlot-based reds as much as cabernet sauvignon-based ones.

'Whether the cool vintages we have had in the late 1990s and early 2000s are a cyclical thing or not, merlot plays more to the region's strengths,' explains winery general manager Ken Christie. 'But cabernet sauvignon will remain vitally important to us.'

Also paramount to Goldwater Estate today is sauvignon blanc, made from Marlborough-grown grapes. It is this wine – and the top quality chardonnay made from Waiheke Island-grown grapes – that are forging this winery's identity for most wine lovers in New Zealand. Not least because greater quantities of these two whites are made than the top-notch reds, but also because of the accessible price.

When Kim and Jeanette Goldwater established their winery the cost of land was not great, says their daughter Gretchen Goldwater.

The winery's first vintage was in 1992 and the biggest growth has been with their Marlborough wine, produced in Blenheim at a winemaking facility in which the Goldwaters are four-way partners. On Waiheke Island, Kim still makes the wine and Jeanette is actively involved at the winery but the daily management is handled by Gretchen and her husband, Ken Christie.

'We all try and say we've got specific roles but in fact it merges as with any small business,' says Christie. 'I'm a general manager in the broadest sense of the term, from being delivery boy, financial controller, IT manager, helping everybody in the day-to-day running … and Jeanette is the person who keeps the team together with her ability to know exactly what's going on.'

Another pioneer winemaker is Stephen White, also known to readers of his tongue-in-cheek wine newsletter as Serge Blanco.

For a long time he made only two reds, the famed and highly sought after Stonyridge Larose and a second tier wine. Larose is a blend of cabernet sauvignon, merlot, malbec, cabernet franc and petit verdot. It rarely fails to impress White's winemaking counterparts in Bordeaux, France. And now that the world realises that a fully ripe, consistently good red wine can be made from grapes grown in New Zealand, White has diversified his range a little to include chardonnay and a blend of grenache, syrah and malbec.

While White and the Goldwaters are the island's wine pioneers, other established vineyards and wineries on Waiheke Island include Te Motu Vineyard, owned and run by the Dunleavy family, Peninsula Estates Wines, Mudbrick Vineyard and Miro Vineyard.

Throughout the 1990s, grape plantings on Waiheke gathered pace until the turn of the millennium. Of the new kids on the Waiheke Island wine block, the best-value top quality red wines often come from Obsidian Vineyard, a joint venture owned by Lindsay Spilman, Andrew Hendry and Chester Nicholls.

The family-owned Stony Batter is making good white wine with its Gravestone Sauvignon Blanc, a subtle wine with textural, grainy and smooth characters derived from lees-stirring, which result in a richly flavoursome sauvignon devoid of the grassy flavours in more southern Kiwi whites.

Stony Batter winery is part of John Spencer's 2200-hectare farm and will possibly become the island's largest wine producer. This means it will be neck and neck, quantity-wise, with Cable Bay Vineyards, owned in part by winemaker Neill Culley.

ABOVE: Iconic Waiheke wine figure Stephen White of Stonyridge Vineyard.
RIGHT: Cable Bay Vineyards, one of Waiheke Island's biggest new ventures, is headed up by Neill and Denise Culley.
FAR RIGHT: Jeanette and Kim Goldwater, who established Goldwater Estate, and whose daughter and son-in-law now help to run the winery.

'It is a ridiculously romantic story. We sailed out here on a Friday night and it took three hours under moonlight. We kids had our PVC raincoats on and we cut tunnels through the gorse on this old rundown farm to plant native trees while the vineyard was being established.' Gretchen Goldwater, Goldwater Estate

Cable Bay is a collection of several vineyards, which is owned in partnership. In this case, viticulturist David Jordan and winemaker Briony McKain are partners with Culley, who makes the wines.

The challenges of growing grapes and making wine on Waiheke relate largely to climate. In 2001 all of the red grapes grown at Goldwater Estate's 14-hectare vineyards were declassified into a lower-priced red wine.

'We have a commitment to keeping that top label up there in quality. If a vintage is not good, we will put the grapes into a lower priced wine and flag the top reds,' says Gretchen Goldwater.

Not all of the island's winemakers are as rigid.

For his first few summers on Waiheke Island, Tony Forsyth says the weather was characterised by dryness everywhere he looked.

'I remember in the mid-1990s the grass being really brown but in the last half decade or more there has been an inexorable change going on with far wetter weather.'

Ken Christie at Goldwater concurs. Conditions on the island in the last half decade have been turbulent and changeable.

Strong winds around fruit-set have knocked back the crop size, reducing the number of grapes on each vine. Merlot, a sensitive grape, has been particularly affected by this unseasonable weather.

'It is nerve-wracking seeing the weather change so dramatically in recent times,' says Christie.

Auckland, Northland and Waiheke Island wineries

Antipodean Farm

Matakana, phone (09) 422 7957

Arahura Vineyard

146 Ness Valley Road, Clevedon, Auckland, phone (09) 292 8749

Ascension Vineyard

480 Matakana Road, Matakana, phone (09) 422 9601

Babich Wines

Babich Road, Henderson, Auckland, phone (09) 833 7859

Brick Bay Wines

Kauri Drive, Sandspit, phone (09) 524 2831

Cable Bay Vineyards

85 Church Bay Road, Waiheke Island, phone (09) 372 5889

Collard Brothers

303 Lincoln Road, Henderson, Auckland, phone (09) 838 8341

Coopers Creek Vineyard

601 State Highway 16, Huapai, Auckland, phone (09) 412 8560

Cottle Hill Winery

Cottle Hill Drive, Kerikeri, phone (09) 407 5203

David Papa Estate Wines

Station Road, Huapai, Auckland, phone (09) 412 9524

Delegat's Wine Estate

172 Hepburn Road, Henderson, Auckland, phone (09) 359 7300

Fenton Estate

56 Korora Road, Oneroa, Waiheke Island, phone (09) 372 2441

Firstland Vineyards

Lyons Road, Pokeno, phone (09) 233 6314

Fullers Vineyard

86 Candia Road, Henderson, Auckland, phone (09) 833 7026

Golden Gate Vineyards

Forest Hill Road, Henderson, Auckland, phone (09) 838 5634

Goldwater Estate

18 Causeway Road, Putiki Bay, Waiheke Island, phone (09) 372 7493

Grandview Wines

172A Don Bucks Road, Henderson, Auckland, phone (09) 833 7176

Harrier Rise Vineyard

748 Waitakere Road, Kumeu, Auckland, phone (09) 412 7256

Heron's Flight Vineyard

49 Sharp Road, Matakana, phone (09) 422 7915

Hyperion Wines

188 Tongue Farm Road, Matakana, phone (09) 422 9375

John Mellars of Great Barrier Island

Great Barrier Island, phone (09) 429 0361

Karaka Point Wines

31 Creek Street, Drury, Auckland, phone (09) 294 7440

Kennedy Point Vineyard

44 Donald Bruce Road, Surfdale, Waiheke, phone (09) 372 5600

Kumeu River Wines

550 State Highway 16, Kumeu, phone (09) 412 8415

Landmark Estate Wines

132 Bruce McLaren Road, Henderson, Auckland,

phone (09) 838 8452

Lincoln Vineyards

130 Lincoln Road, Henderson, Auckland, phone (09) 838 6944

Longview Wine Estate

State Highway 1, Otaika, Whangarei, phone (09) 438 7277

Mahurangi Estate Winery

Hamilton Road, Warkworth, phone (09) 425 0306

Marsden Estate

Wiroa Road, Kerikeri, phone (09) 407 9398

Matakana Estate

568 Matakana Road, Matakana, phone (09) 425 0494

Matua Valley Wines

Waikoukou Valley Road, Waimauku, Auckland, phone (09 411 8301

Mazuran's Vineyard

255 Lincoln Road, Henderson, Auckland, phone (09) 838 6945

Montana Wines

171 Pilkington Road, Glen Innes, Auckland, phone (09) 570 8400

Mother's Cellar

329 Lincoln Road, Henderson, Auckland, phone (09) 838 8362

Mudbrick Vineyard/Shepherd's Point Vineyard

Church Bay Road, Oneroa, Waiheke Island, phone (09) 372 9050

Nobilo Wine Group

45 Station Road, Huapai, Auckland, phone (09) 366 0030

Obsidian Vineyard

Te Makiri Road, Onetangi, Waiheke Island, phone (09) 372 6100

Odyssey Wines

Henderson, Auckland, phone (09) 837 5410

Okahu Estate Vineyard and Winery

Okahu Road, Okahu, Kaitaia, phone (09) 408 0888

Omata Estate

Aucks Road, Russell, Bay of Islands, phone (09) 403 8007

Onetangi Road Vineyard

82 Onetangi Road, Waiheke Island, phone (09) 372 6130

Pacific Vineyards

90 McLeod Road, Henderson, Auckland, phone (09) 838 9578

Passage Rock Wines

438 Orapiu Road, Te Matuku Bay, Waiheke Island, phone (09) 372 7257

Peninsula Estate Wines

52A Korora Road, Oneroa, Waiheke Island, phone (09) 372 7866

Pleasant Valley Wines

322 Henderson Valley Road, Henderson, Auckland,
phone (09) 838 8857

Providence Vineyard

Cnr Omaha Flats Road and Takatu Road, Matakana,
phone (09) 444 6064

Puriri Hills

Arcadia Farm, 398 North Road, Clevedon, Auckland,
phone (09) 292 9264

Putiki Bay Vineyards

84 Vintage Lane, Te Whau Point, Waiheke Island,
phone (09) 372 7322

Ransom Wines

Valerie Close, Warkworth, phone (09) 425 8862

St Jerome Wines

219 Metcalfe Road, Henderson, Auckland, phone (09) 833 6205

St Nesbit Winery

Hingaia Road, Papakura, Auckland, phone (09) 298 5057

Saratoga Estate

72 Onetangi Road, Waiheke Island, phone (09) 372 6450

Seibel Wines

113 Sturges Road, Henderson, Auckland, phone (09) 836 6113

Soljans Wines

State Highway 16, Kumeu, Auckland, phone (09) 412 5858

Stony Batter Estate

Man-O-War Farms, Waiheke Island, phone (09) 372 9649

Stonyridge Vineyard

87 Onetangi Road, Onetangi, Waiheke Island, phone (09) 372 8822

Te Whau Vineyard

218 Te Whau Drive, Te Whau Peninsula, Waiheke Island,
phone (09) 372 7191

Villa Maria Wines

118 Montgomerie Road, Mangere, Auckland, phone (09) 255 0660

Vin Alto

424 Creightons Road, Clevedon, Auckland, phone (09) 292 8845

Vodanovich Wines

229 Lincoln Road, Henderson, Auckland, phone (09) 836 2855

Waiheke Vineyards

Onetangi Road, Onetangi, Waiheke Island, phone (09) 486 3859

Waimarie Wines

234 Muriwai Valley Road, Waimauku, Auckland,
phone (09) 411 9983

West Brook Winery

215 Ararimu Valley Road, Waimauku, Auckland,
phone (09) 411 9924

Gisborne

Gisborne is New Zealand's third largest and most isolated winemaking region, a place where the locals languish in sunny seclusion, claiming the title chardonnay capital of New Zealand and producing a quirky array of top tasting whites, from gewürztraminer and muscat to the country's best viognier. Most wine from grapes grown here has been made in bulk, with only a handful of top-notch drops. Contract grape-growers have something to answer for, says winemaker James Millton, who is pleased to see a paradigm shift in the thinking of many of Gisborne's winemakers.

The Gisborne wine scene can best be summed up in two 'm' words: Montana and Millton.

Montana is the largest winemaking company in the country while Millton is one of the smallest – and also one of the most important wine companies in the world. Winemaker James Millton is one of the most influential pioneers globally of biodynamic grape-growing and winemaking practices. In itself this should be enough to make Gisborne of paramount importance in the New Zealand wine scene, but this region has long been disparaged because of the tendency for contract growers to supply vast quantities of grapes to large wine companies for bulk winemaking.

Change is afoot and it is being led by Montana, which not only makes large volumes of wine but also top quality gewürztraminer and chardonnay from this region.

Gisborne encompasses the North Island east coast roughly from East Cape south to Mahia Peninsula, much of it hill country with a limited area for grape-growing. Most of the activity takes place on the valley floor of the Poverty Bay flats, behind the sun drenched coastal city of Gisborne. On these rich alluvial plains grow all manner of horticultural and other crops, as well as grapes.

But Gisborne is an edgy place to grow grapes for winemaking, as viticulturist Joe Corban discovered in 1968.

Sunshine and warmth are plentiful commodities in this most easterly of all New Zealand's grape-growing regions and its soils can be relatively fertile, but therein lies the rub.

PREVIOUS PAGES: Most of Gisborne's grapes are grown on the Poverty Bay flats, near to the city, which sits on the edge of the east coast. This is the third biggest winemaking region in New Zealand.
ABOVE: Gisborne winemaker James Millton has always been interested in fermenting fruit, something he was expelled from high school for doing. Now he and his wife Annie are the most famous of all Gisborne winemakers.
RIGHT: Millton Vineyards on a misty morning in early summer. Most of the vines are grown organically with a growing proportion being treated to biodynamic growing techniques.

Corban, now in his seventies, was one of the first modern wine pioneers in Gisborne when he and other Corban family members purchased land here and planted grapes.

'In Auckland it would take us four years to plant a vine and have it come to fruition, and if we'd used müller-thurgau we'd get three to four tonnes to the acre in the fourth year,' explains Corban, who adds that in Gisborne the Corban family winery would get 12 to 15 tonnes of grapes to the acre for chardonnay. 'And that was in vineyards that were just two to three years old,' he says now, several decades on but still taken aback by the unexpected lushness of this region.

Gisborne's modern day wine reputation was built on the back of high yielding grapevines and predominantly bulk wine production. It was never the intention of the first modern winemakers in the region, in the 1970s and 1980s, to make bulk wine, but the temptation to turn vast quantities of fast growing grapes into wine for immediate consumption was strong.

Ironically, it is this bulk winemaking mentality – from both the winemakers and the marketplace – that has now led to a shift in thinking on the part of Montana Wines, the region's largest producer.

'Our region gets slammed for having low quality and high yields but that's exactly what the wine companies want, so not only do the grape-growers have something to answer for, those who drink the wine do as well,' says Gisborne winemaker James Millton.

The first winemakers in Gisborne arrived by accident in 1850 when Marist missionaries landed at Turanganui and planted vines before heading off again, to their original intended destination of Hawke's Bay.

Gisborne's second wave of winemaking was at the beginning of the twentieth century, when German-born Friedrich Wohnsiedler planted grapevines at Waihirere. For decades he made wine after anti-German prejudice around the time of the First World War resulted in the destruction of his Gisborne pork butchery – as well as the nationwide renaming of German sausage to Belgian sausage. By the 1960s, Wohnsiedler was making 95,000 gallons of wine annually, but gradually his business was taken over. His name lives on in one of the country's most affordable but innocuous white wines, Montana Wohnsiedler.

'The contract growers here are doing the exact job that the wine companies require, in producing as many grapes per vine as possible, but having said that, Montana Wines is lifting the quality profile so that the perception of this region is sure to change.'

James Millton

Chardonnay reigns supreme in Gisborne, as its most widely planted variety, making up 56 percent of the region's vintage area in 2003. It is expected that chardonnay will remain the dominant variety, with a predicted overall increase in the number of vines planted in the Gisborne region of about six percent by 2005.

Some winemakers in the region are pinning their hopes on newly introduced grapes albarino and petit mansang; these aromatic white wine varieties, according to winemaker James Millton, should respond positively to the growing conditions a maritime climate like Gisborne's has to offer.

White grape varieties have produced the most impressive Gisborne wines to date, most notably chardonnay, gewürztraminer,

LEFT: The Milltons' seven-hectare Riverpoint Vineyard, planted in chardonnay and viognier grapes, is in the Matawhero area, near Denis Irwin's once-famous gewürztraminer vineyard.
ABOVE LEFT AND RIGHT: The climate in Gisborne is warm but also sometimes a little humid, throwing up a challenge to winemakers like James Millton, pictured right, who are growing their vines in an environmentally sustainable manner, without the use of commercial fungicides, which he believes are not the most effective way to stop disease in the vineyard.

müller-thurgau and now, in tiny quantities, viognier. Several red wine grape varieties have always been grown in Gisborne but with only specialised success. The most planted red is currently merlot, with pinot noir and syrah being the next most planted red grape varieties. The early ripening malbec grape is being pressed into service to make soft textured, early drinking reds, a wine style well suited to the region's long summers.

The growth in the region is predicted to be made up mostly of merlot, chardonnay, gewürztraminer and sémillon. It is also expected that müller-thurgau, which accounts for eight percent of the region's vineyards, will decline significantly with the remaining palomino and flora grapes – used as workhorse varieties in bulk winemaking – to be removed entirely.

Soft, tropical fruit flavoured chardonnays made from grapes grown in Gisborne are produced by tiny Gisborne-based wineries as well as many of New Zealand's largest wineries. Montana Wines in Gisborne produces vast quantities of chardonnay across the gamut of price brackets but many wineries outside the region also make chardonnay from grapes grown in Gisborne. Babich Wines, Lincoln Vineyards and Matua Valley Wines are producers of consistently top quality chardonnays from the lowest price right up to super premium wines, with higher priced tags accordingly.

When it is grown on silt-loam soils, as the region's, and the country's, best aromatic wines (gewürztraminer, muscat, viognier) are, chardonnay has the ability to improve with age for several years. But chardonnay's innate youthful appeal and beautiful drinkability when young mean that little wine is left in the cellars of the region's wineries to age spectacularly.

This is pertinent for Gisborne's wine scene in particular, and for New Zealand's as a whole, in its quest to find the best places in which to grow and make great white wines.

Then again, some Gisborne wines are made with early drinking in mind, and when its grapes are grown on predominantly clay-based soils, Gisborne chardonnay becomes an immediately approachable wine with a forward, 'drink me and drink me now' personality.

No longer just a bulk wine or cheap white wine producing region – that is how Gisborne is increasingly being seen, thanks to James and Annie Millton, who have cemented their reputation as the most quality driven winery in the region and one of the most significant in the country.

The Millton Vineyard was the first to gain full organic certification in New Zealand (1986) and is now the most dedicated follower of

ABOVE: Bill Irwin and his son Denis Irwin's Matawhero Vineyard showed early on that good gewürztraminer had a home in Gisborne.
RIGHT: Nets are commonplace in vineyards throughout New Zealand just as the grapes begin their most important ripening time, veraison, when the sugars and acids change most dramatically.

biodynamic viticultural practices. These involve a lot more than just the perceived mumbo-jumbo that James Millton claims most people associate with the biodynamic philosophy.

The Millton Vineyard consistently makes brilliantly focused white wines, ranging from riesling and muscat to full-bodied chardonnay and the best viognier in the country. Throw a chenin blanc into the mix and the picture is one of adventuresome, brave winemaking on a relatively small scale but one that has wowed not only organic winemakers around the world but wine lovers too.

Montana Wines is also making top quality wines as well as large quantities of everyday drinking wine. Aside from these two wineries, there is a smattering of other, mostly small, wine producers in Gisborne, like Amor-Bendall, that make top quality wine.

Wineries like these are largely reliant on the facilities of Millton or Montana to make their wines and they do not have cellar doors for tourists to visit or buy wine from.

'If there was higher tourist traffic in Gisborne, the region would have had more small wineries established in the area with a greater emphasis on high quality table wine,' says Montana Wines chief winemaker Jeff Clarke, who attributes lack of tourist numbers to Gisborne's relative isolation.

'It is a shame we don't see more tourists go there or more winery cellar doors open because now that we are changing the varietal mix from the bulk producing grape varieties, which formed the mainstay of the early production, to higher quality varieties, Gisborne has a future as a quality wine producer.'

Even Clarke admits that only time will tell just how high that quality can possibly be.

'Whether Gisborne can become a producer of predominantly super premium table wines remains to be seen but we are making top wines in the premium range and we see good signs in both our new vineyards and selected established ones that point to top quality wine production.'

James Millton readily confesses that he raises more questions than he answers when asked about winemaking.

Speaking on a chilly Auckland day in winter, 2003, New Zealand's leading proponent of organic and biodynamic winemaking reveals little

about the methods he uses to grow grapes and make wine the biodynamic way.

'I am trying to get away from the certified organic cross that we have been bearing for so many years now because what matters – what has always mattered the most – is that we are making good quality wines.'

Quality is a moving target for Millton. On the 1.2 hectare Naboth's Vineyard, where the grapes for his top wines are planted, there is no irrigation and no use of herbicides, systemic chemicals or fungicides. It is a fully biodynamic vineyard. Yet there is no barcode on the back on the bottles of wine made from grapes grown here and there is nothing on their labels to say that they are organically certified. Instead, on the pinot noirs and chardonnays from this vineyard, which are named Clos de Ste Anne (a tribute to his wife, Annie), it says simply: 'biodynamically grown grapes'.

While many of Millton's wines have the official New Zealand Bio-Gro certification, these biodynamically grown wines do not, because the country's Demeter Certification (the only certification for biodynamics) does not have wine certification yet. And even if it did, Millton says it would be a token gesture to mention such certification on the bottle.

'Biodynamics cannot be instructed to you, it is something you have to do yourself,' he says.

'People say to me, "It must be hard growing grapes in Gisborne" because of some simple idea about the climate and I also get a lot of comments that "Your wines are really good even though they are organic". Instead of getting into long-winded explanations, I just say, "Thank you".'

Millton describes biodynamics as creating a situation that is at ease with or in harmony with the natural environment as opposed to one that is controlled, combative and has dis-harmony or is dis-eased. But he, like the others, still has to combat fungus, which he describes as a natural progression of the life energy of a vineyard.

'Fungus is nature's messenger that all is not well. We deal with that by balancing the silica and the calcium in the soil to achieve the right balance both in summer and winter.'

The Milltons' first commercial vintage was in 1984. When they returned from overseas, the couple took over existing vineyards owned by Annie's father, one of the first contract grape-growers in the region, which were planted in müller-thurgau, pinotage and chenin blanc.

'I told my father-in-law we couldn't look after his vineyards unless I could plant some decent grapes,' says Millton, who covertly replanted

LEFT: Pinot noir grapes fermenting at vintage time. Although the majority of New Zealand pinot noirs have come from the South Island, Gisborne winemaker James Millton is now crafting his own from grapes grown on a small hillside vineyard.
ABOVE: Bins of grapes at harvest time must be processed swiftly before the next lot come in, even at a large winery like Montana Wines in Gisborne, where three wineries have been amalgamated into one vast and efficient production line.

what were then deemed to be experimental grape varieties in selected rows bar the last 10 vines at the bottom of the row that could be seen from the road when driving past. Within a year his father-in-law realised that James was determined, and soon after the remaining areas were replanted.

At the same time, Annie, a trained florist, was growing flowers and herbs underneath the vines, which gave both her and James an insight into how companion planting has an effect on grapes.

'It's not as if we set out to develop this business. We were just a couple of kids playing around but things got serious pretty quickly,' explains Millton.

Soon he and Annie were intentionally planting companion plants and flowers alongside grapevines to improve the health of the plants. It seemed, Millton says, to be putting themselves in other people's hands if they had followed all the advice of the chemical company representatives without question.

'Instead we chose to try to understand nature and looking at it logically you see there is little or no need for chemical intervention. It is about understanding the rhythm of nature.'

Put another way, Millton says biodynamics has meant he does not have to climb over the mountain that he sees in front of him. 'Biodynamics shows you can walk around it to get to the other side, where you need to be.'

At Gisborne's biggest winery, Montana Wines, things are not the polar opposite many wine drinkers might expect them to be to Millton's clean, green image.

The meeting room at Montana's Gisborne winery is lined with large images of Friedrich Wohnsiedler and his family. They are a tribute to Wohnsiedler, says their owner, winery manager Roger McLernon who, for many, is synonymous with Montana's Gisborne operation.

McLernon cares for Montana Wines as though he owned the company and no wonder, given that he has worked for them for several decades. In that time, he has observed Montana Wines grow from one winery to the complex operation it is today, which encompasses three working wineries linked by 14 stainless steel pipes that travel seven kilometres on their journey from crushing to tank and barrel.

In the early 1990s, Montana Wines was crushing 200 tonnes of grapes a day during vintage and in 2003 that figure had grown to around 1000 tonnes a day, with Montana Wines responsible for 74 percent of Gisborne's total wine production. Because of the winery's complex infrastructure and economies of scale, it can and will nearly

ABOVE: It's easy for drinkers to forget that wine is made in the vineyard but winemakers constantly remind themselves of this fact, surrounded as they are by equipment to tend their vines, as here at the Milltons' Naboth Vineyard.
RIGHT ABOVE: Keeping birds at bay as grapes ripen means work laying netting.
RIGHT FAR ABOVE: Piles of wire for vineyard trellising at Matawhero Wines.
RIGHT BELOW: A view from Naboth's Vineyard in Gisborne.

double its production with very little capital expenditure, explains Montana Gisborne chief winemaker Steve Voysey.

Voysey says he and other winemakers are more rigorous about where they grow and source grapes now than they were in the past.

'We have found that by careful selection of grapes and further lifting the game in our best vineyards that we can make improvements in our premium and super premium wines.'

For the future, he hopes small amounts of top gewürztraminer from selected vineyards can be of high quality but does not see a large market for the voluptuous tasting, difficult to pronounce gewürztraminer grape.

As evidence of that, Voysey has to make 17 or 18 different chardonnays and just three gewürztraminers. However, both varieties are growing in production for Montana Wines.

New Zealand's most stylish example of gewürztraminer used to be produced by Gisborne winemaker Bill Irwin and later by his son, Denis Irwin. In 2003 Montana Wines bought a large block of the Matawhero Vineyard from Denis Irwin, in which it plans to plant gewürztraminer vines.

Whether the new gewürztraminer vines will produce wines at the super premium level is not yet known, but Voysey is excited by the Matawhero vineyard site that they are replanting. Its promise lies not merely in its history of holding great old gewürztraminers, but in the relatively cool, free-draining soils, compared with the heavier clays that many of Montana's gewürztraminers have been grown on.

Replanting the old Matawhero vineyard will help Montana Wines to harness some of the fresher, more Turkish delight type flavours that the gewürztraminer grape can express.

'The future of Gisborne is in winemakers identifying better clones of suitable grapes like gewürztraminer and other varieties like viognier and pinot gris.'

Steve Voysey, Montana Gisborne chief winemaker

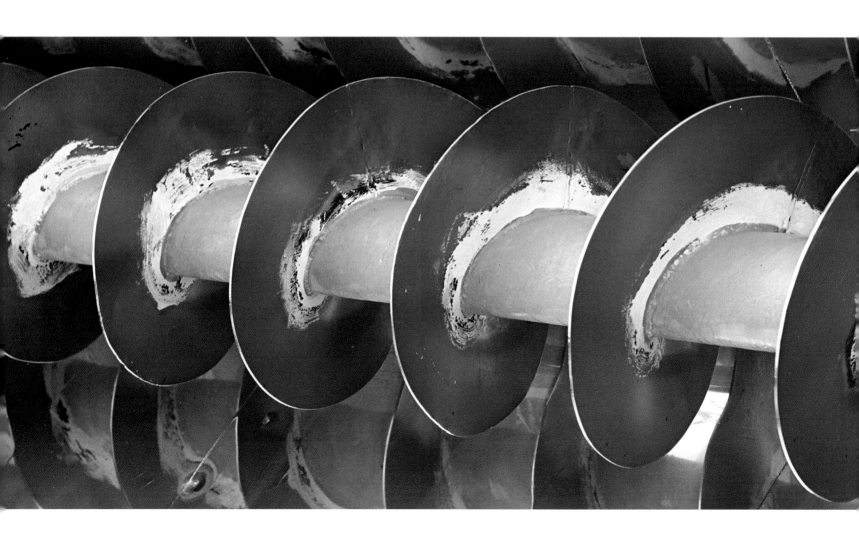

'It's a steep learning curve figuring out which soils best suit which grapes and it will take a lot longer than just a few years because we need to evaluate mature vines rather than very young ones,' explains Voysey.

He and the winemaking team at Montana's Gisborne winery are also expanding their production of chardonnay for both table wine and sparkling wine as well as planting more pinot gris and their first viognier grapes.

Viognier is not easy, says James Millton. 'That's typical of us. We always choose the hardest grapes,' he says, with a wry laugh.

'First it was with chenin blanc, then riesling and muscat – which nobody thinks they like till they try ours – and now it is with the very seductive charms of the viognier grape, which makes a wine that encompasses the lightness and aroma of riesling with the spicy taste of gewürztraminer and the full-bodied appeal of chardonnay.'

Not that he has success with viognier every single vintage. Like gewürztraminer, viognier is a sensitive grape and if the season is cool or windy (not usually a big problem in Gisborne) it will yield tiny amounts of grapes.

LEFT: Montana Wines in Gisborne is a finely polished operation, processing thousands of tonnes of grapes every year and a wide range of varieties.
BELOW LEFT: Cleaning out tanks at Montana Wines in Gisborne, in preparation for a record vintage.
BELOW RIGHT: Winemakers take a tank sample of gewürztraminer for tasting.

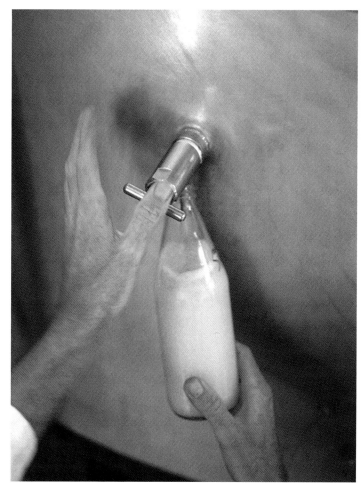

Millton also plans to import new clones of chenin blanc to New Zealand because he says that the clones of the much-maligned chenin blanc variety that are currently available here were originally imported for their ability to produce quantity rather than quality wine.

As for red wine varieties, for most of its wine history Gisborne has yielded mainly mediocre merlot grapes, while with its cabernets (sauvignon and franc) there has often been, and sometimes still is, a slightly herbal taste.

Moreover, there has been precious little pinot noir, syrah or red grapes planted until recently. Most of the region's winemakers and grape-growers are using Gisborne's red grapes purely as blending components in multi-regional wines that they produce or else in reds that are relatively light.

But now that the region's best winemakers have been rewarded for their work with white wines, the quest has begun to perfect pinot noir and other reds.

Pinot noir is to a winemaker what a mountain is to a mountaineer, says James Millton, adding that, like Everest was to Sir Edmund Hillary, pinot noir is for most winemakers.

'The way that many of us feel about pinot noir is that we just want to "knock the bastard off" and make a great one.'

For his part, Millton says he plans to make a pinot noir with a powerful style from the grapes that he and Annie grow on their unusually steep hillside slope in Gisborne.

When he returned from pinot noir's spiritual home of Burgundy, France, in 2001, Millton says he realised that pinot noir requires as much attention in the winery as it does in the vineyard, where it is notoriously difficult to grow.

'I had always tried to be as natural as possible in my approach to pinot noir but I suddenly realised after my trip to France that I had to get back to basics, and do very winemaker type things like use enzymes and new barrels to see what would happen.'

What has happened is that James Millton now makes better pinot noir and he still focuses strongly on growing grapes without added irrigation or any of the sprays he rejects for the tiny hillside slope that is Naboth's Vineyard.

'In the next five years I would like to see all of New Zealand's vineyards become an ecological viticultural appellation, which means that we all need to strongly limit the use of soluble fertilisers and enhance the use of compost and microbes that we use to feed the vitality of the soil.'

ABOVE: In the 1960s Corbans and Montana Wines contracted local growers to raise grapes, thus getting the modern era of grape-growing in the region underway. Today Montana Wines is by far the largest winery in Gisborne and is set to stay that way.

Gisborne wineries

Amor-Bendall Wines

145 Wairere Road, Wainui Beach, Gisborne, phone 021 859 435

Gisborne Wine Company

Kaiti Beach Road, Gisborne, phone (06) 863 1285

Matawhero Wines

Riverpoint Road, Matawhero, Gisborne, phone (06) 868 8366

Millton Vineyard

Papatu Road, Manutuke, Gisborne, phone (06) 862 8680

Montana Wines

Solander Street, Gisborne, phone (06) 867 9819

Pouparae Park

385 Bushmere Road, Gisborne, phone (06) 867 7931

Shalimar Estate Winery

Ngatapa Road, RD 2, Gisborne, phone (06) 862 7776

Thorpe Brothers Wines

Lytton Road, Gisborne, phone (06) 863 0623

Tiritiri Organic Vineyard

1646 Waimata Valley Road, Gisborne, phone (06) 867 0372

TW Wines

Back Ormond Road, RD 1, Hexton, Gisborne, phone (06) 868 6199

Vinoptima

138 Ngakoroa Road, Ormond, Gisborne, phone (06) 353 6565

Waimata Vineyard

Upper Stout Street, Gisborne, phone (06) 867 2010

Waiohika Estate

75 Waimata Valley Road, Gisborne, phone (06) 867 4670

Wrights Wines

c/- The Works, Kaiti Beach Road, Gisborne, phone (06) 868 0967

Hawke's Bay

It is very easy to love Hawke's Bay wine. Chardonnay, cabernet sauvignon and merlot rule the roost here, with local winemakers consistently turning out some of New Zealand's most stylish wines from these three varieties. They are also fine-tuning gewürztraminer, riesling, sauvignon blanc and pinot noir as well as experimenting with warmer-climate grapes like viognier, syrah, montepulciano and tempranillo. It's not that they are trying to be all things to all people, rather that Hawke's Bay's winemakers have diverse growing conditions that allow a broad range of grape varieties to flourish.

No matter which way you look at it, John Kemble's new Hawke's Bay winery is enormously impressive, both in its physical stature and in the philosophy behind the building.

The two-building structure is approached by a circular driveway that lies on top of two underground wine cellars. Eventually, these underground caves will house at least 4000 barrels of wine and be linked by a tunnel, allowing easy access between the two barrel halls and the buildings above. Above the ground are the winemaking and administration facilities, a winery restaurant and luxuriously spacious winery accommodation from which visitors get a sweeping view of the 80 hectares of vines grown here.

Yes, Kemblefield Estate is big. Its inland location at Mangatahi makes it one of the more controversial sub-regions within the diverse climatic and soil conditions in the Hawke's Bay wine region because it is relatively cool.

Here, planted on gravelly, free-draining terraces, are chardonnay, merlot, cabernet sauvignon, sauvignon blanc, malbec, cabernet franc, sémillon, pinot gris and gewürztraminer. Trailing all of these is a small smattering of zinfandel, a variety Kemble had experience with in California prior to emigrating to New Zealand.

Unlike the other wines made at Kemblefield Estate, zinfandel is not produced every year because, Kemble says, it's mainly for fun that he makes it and not every vintage is warm enough to produce it.

Kemble settled in Hawke's Bay because of the versatile growing conditions. 'And because it was more affordable to set up in New Zealand than in California,' he adds, with a chuckle.

PREVIOUS PAGES: Autumn leaves on a vineyard in the Gimblett Gravels district, one of Hawke's Bay's biggest viticultural assets. The Bay is full of sub-regions displaying various climatic conditions and soil types, and the Gravels is one of the hottest areas in a relatively cool climate.
ABOVE: Crates at vintage time at a Hawke's Bay winery.
RIGHT: The Esk Valley is one of the Bay's northernmost areas of vineyards and is planted, like the rest of the region, in an array of different grape varieties, including chardonnay, riesling, sauvignon blanc, cabernet sauvignon, cabernet franc and merlot, among others.

Kemblefield Estate winery is typical of wineries in Hawke's Bay today in that it is producing consistently good wines across a wide range of different varieties.

In the second half of the 1990s and the first few years of the new millennium, many of the wineries established in the Bay were set up by international wine lovers, often in a joint operation with the locals but sometimes alone. Of these new ventures, Craggy Range is the largest and Sileni Estate (a New Zealand-owned winery) is another vast operation; both were established from day one with more than enough capital to give them a head start on competitors.

Hawke's Bay is the most diverse wine region in New Zealand climatically.

The region's stretch begins in the north at Wairoa, reaching down to Woodville and to the northern boundary of the Wairarapa, taking in an enviable and challenging array of different altitudes, distances from the sea and soil changes along the way. The great variety of grapes being grown and trialled in the Bay is a reflection of the region's varying climates and terrains.

In the north of Hawke's Bay grapevines grow near Wairoa, Raupunga and Nuhaka but most of the region's vineyards are planted on the sprawling, flat Heretaunga Plains. Vineyards grow in every direction out from Napier city: north at Eskdale; further inland to the cooler climes of the Dartmoor Valley; in the slightly warmer areas of Taradale and Meeanee.

The hottest sub-region for growing grapes in the Bay is the Gimblett Road area, which is New Zealand's second delineated grape-growing area, known as Gimblett Gravels. South of Gimblett Road, a pocket of particularly warm grape-growing land exists near Havelock North.

At present, there are three wineries and several vineyards on the coast at Te Awanga along with a smattering of experimental small vineyard blocks planted south of the Heretaunga Plains.

While Hawke's Bay's climate is more versatile for growing grapes than any other New Zealand wine region, it is also a haven for those who love beaches, vast tracts of flat land and clean rivers and who do not mind the fact that the nearest large city, Wellington, is about four hours' drive to the south.

Viticulturally, changes have been dramatic in the last decade. The most significant difference has been to the line-up of the region's red grape varieties.

As if to herald a new era of winemaking with the turn of the century, merlot overtook cabernet sauvignon in 2000 as the most widely planted red grape in the Bay and in New Zealand.

Syrah vines are growing in number and as a wine it is gaining fans both nationally and internationally, especially for wine drinkers who long ago tired of over-ripe 'shiraz' and have been searching for wines with the subtlety of Hawke's Bay syrahs.

Then there is montepulciano, tempranillo, sangiovese and gamay noir, plantings of which are tiny. The most important change is the fact that merlot is now predominant.

'We ignored merlot at our peril for too long,' says Tony Prichard, Hawke's Bay's regional winemaker for Montana Wines.

'As we became more exposed to international markets, people started looking harder for the answer to why our cabernet-based reds tasted grassy.'

The answer for many winemakers, including Prichard, was to plant more merlot. His relatively newfound respect for the merlot grape is based on many factors, including the fact that merlot ripens earlier and has a more forgiving nature than cabernet sauvignon when it comes to expressing the flavours that come with being grown in a cool climate.

'That very green character that used to be prevalent in New Zealand reds is known as methoxypyrazine and it is rare to taste it in merlot while in cabernet sauvignon it is common, especially in cool climates,' explains Prichard.

Prichard diplomatically adds that cabernet sauvignon is still of enormous importance but just not taking the leading role in all of the Bay's red wines today.

Hawke's Bay is an easy place in which to find winemakers like this, who realised relatively recently that merlot was easier to grow than cabernet sauvignon in most of the soils in the Bay region.

The cabernet sauvignon versus merlot debate rages on.

It is a hard call coming up with the best red grape for Hawke's Bay, says Esk Valley winemaker Gordon Russell, who is an advocate for merlot.

'Until recently I would have categorically said merlot but I also think malbec seems ideally suited to the region.'

While the world is waiting, wine drinkers can expect a huge leap forward in the quality of red wines that have poured out of Hawke's Bay over the last half decade and more.

LEFT: At the small Unison Vineyard, owned by Anna-Barbara and Bruce Helliwell. It's the sun on the stones that gets many Hawke's Bay-based winemakers all hot and bothered, as the warmth speeds up the ripening process in vines.
ABOVE: Lunch in the sun at Terroir with the dramatic backdrop of Te Mata Peak. Terroir is the winery restaurant at the relatively new Craggy Range Vineyards.

BELOW LEFT: Te Mata Estate Winery's flagship red is Coleraine, made mostly from cabernet sauvignon.
BELOW RIGHT: Peter Cowley, winemaker and part-owner of Te Mata Estate Winery, which is one of the most established in the region with an unerring focus on creating top quality chardonnay and cabernet sauvignon-dominant red wines.
RIGHT: Barrels on the move at Craggy Range Vineyards, which has two operational wineries in Hawke's Bay.

'Merlot is always going to be the base of the Hawke's Bay red wine industry because it is less demanding than either cabernet or syrah,' says Steve Smith from Craggy Range Vineyards.

Having said that, Smith expects that the Bay's best red wines will still be made predominantly from cabernet sauvignon.

'Cabernet sauvignon has more of a feeling of greatness than merlot's generous richness and forwardness. Where merlot is concerned, what you see is what you get, but with cabernet sauvignon, it's all about complexity and an X-factor.'

The French grape gamay appealed to Hawke's Bay winemaker Peter Cowley because, he says, it is one of those varieties that when turned into wine you think, 'My god, this is delicious.'

It's exactly that X-factor that Cowley is now bottling as Te Mata's Woodthorpe Gamay Noir.

'Cabernet sauvignon is the most site-specific grape in the region, which means that it will perform well or badly more obviously than any other grapes just because of where it is grown in Hawke's Bay.'   Peter Cowley, winemaker, Te Mata Estate

As the long-time maker of some of New Zealand's top reds, Te Mata's Coleraine and Awatea, Cowley seems one of the least likely people to make a red that is generally considered to be like a white wine drinker's red wine. However, good gamay works so well as stand-alone wine that Cowley says it is a refreshing change from using oak barrels.

'There is no problem ripening gamay in Hawke's Bay and what started out as a fun little aside has turned into such a tasty wine that we are growing production a little each year now,' says Cowley.

Then there is tempranillo, which ex-pat Australian winemaker John Hancock, one of the owners and winemakers at Trinity Hill winery on State Highway 50, first made in 1990. It's a relatively early ripening, traditional Spanish grape variety. When grown in Hawke's Bay, tempranillo develops tastes that are very similar to how they are in their homeland: savoury and robust with a stewed fruit flavour too.

'It's the perfect grape for blending, which is what they do with it most of the time in Spain,' says Hancock, who may blend it with another red grape in the long term.

'It is good to have something out of the ordinary to choose to drink, so perhaps the last thing we should be thinking of doing is blending after all,' says Hancock.

The big taste improvement in wines made from grapes grown in Hawke's Bay in recent times has been due largely to better site selection, vineyard management, cropping levels and timing of harvest and irrigation management.

While most wineries in the region have spent the better part of the last decade refining these practices, one of the most striking cabernet sauvignon-based reds made in the country has been at Te Mata Estate.

'Some of the first Hawke's Bay wines I tasted were the McWilliam's Cabernets from the 1960s and, ever since then, I have always felt that Hawke's Bay has great potential with classic Bordeaux grape varieties,' says Cowley.

'For us the strongest red grape is cabernet sauvignon, when it is grown in the right places. The dark fruits and taut tannins give the wines an ageing potential that is hard to achieve without cabernet sauvignon and the good wines get better with age.'

Every year Te Mata Elston Chardonnay proves the point that Hawke's Bay is the home of New Zealand's best full-bodied white wines. This wine sits alongside a growing stable of other top quality chardonnays made in the Bay, including Babich Irongate Chardonnay.

Gewürztraminer, which usually requires different conditions to chardonnay, also thrives in some parts of the Bay.

The family-owned Babich Wines was one of the first to plant grapes on the Gimblett Gravels, where they grow gewürztraminer.

'When we first bought land there in the 1980s, people told us we were crazy,' recalls Peter Babich, with a wry smile.

'We just knew how good this area was and we only regret now that we didn't buy 400 acres instead of the 90 acres we got hold of.'

Peter's son, David, who now manages the Auckland-based Babich Wines, is surprised that the sensitive gewürztraminer grape thrives on these soils alongside a host of better known, better liked and easier to grow grapes like chardonnay, cabernet sauvignon, syrah, malbec, merlot, pinotage and cabernet franc.

'Gewürztraminer is tough to grow because it crops erratically, so we only make tiny quantities of it and crop them at very low levels, which is a factor of this finicky grape anyway.'

What happens, he says, is that they leave their gewürztraminer hanging out on the vines for longer than may be usual, until they notice what he describes as a bloom in flavour.

'We're not just looking at the physiological ripeness because true ripeness is about a mix of things: what grape acids are doing, what the brix are doing and how that flavour profile changes just prior to harvesting the grapes.'

Like most winemakers growing grapes in this region, Babich Wines is best known for its cabernet sauvignon and chardonnay. Its wines made from these varieties constitute its largest production and deliver the best wines in the broad Babich stable.

Which grape varieties are most suited to the future of winemaking in Hawke's Bay? Ask Steve Smith and the viticulturist says that things keep changing.

'At one time syrah seemed like just a glimmer but now, when this grape is grown on certain sites, syrah will make a major impact on the New Zealand wine industry,' says the Master of Wine and general manager of Craggy Range Vineyards.

New Zealand's answer to the sea of Australian shiraz that has washed onto our shores for the last decade is to grow a more subtle version of the same grape and call it by the French name, syrah.

The reputation of New Zealand syrah is out of all proportion to the measly amount that is grown. In 1994, just 16 hectares was planted, which has grown to a still puny 144 hectares.

'Better vineyard site selection and older vines as well as better understanding of growing grapes in our soils have all contributed to developing red wines of world class standard, as results internationally are starting to show.'   Rod McDonald, Vidal Estate

Steve Smith says he would prefer to see the volume of red wines reduced in order to allow the merlot grape to express itself as well as possible in the region's best red wines.

Then there is pinot noir. It is the fifth most planted grape in the region, used both to make still table wine and as a component in sparkling wine.

Just as this book was nearing completion, one of the region's biggest syrah producers sent two new pinot noirs onto the market as ambassadors of cool climate vineyards that are relatively new to southern Hawke's Bay.

Trinity Hill winemakers Warren Gibson and John Hancock have been working with pinot noir in the Bay since 1990. And since 2000, they have made small amounts of pinot noir from new clones on a vineyard that they helped to develop on the coast at Te Awanga.

ABOVE: Merlot is the second most planted grape variety in Hawke's Bay with 24 percent of the region's vineyard area.
RIGHT: Winemaker John Hancock, the hands-on owner of Trinity Hill on State Highway 50, is an experimentalist, growing grapes like montepulciano and tempranillo as well as all the popular varieties.

New Zealand's oldest winery is Te Mata Estate. The brick stable that Bernard Chambers, son of a Te Mata sheep farmer, built in 1872 was restyled into his working winery in 1895. It still stands in use as a cask storage room at Te Mata Estate today. It is not known precisely when Chambers first planted grapes in Hawke's Bay but in 1892 he acquired his vines from the Marist missionaries who established the region's first vineyard, Mission Vineyards, which is still in operation today. Father Lampila and the two lay brothers, Florentin and Basil, mistakenly landed at Gisborne, in Poverty Bay, before hotfooting it on to their intended destination, Hawke's Bay. In 1851 they planted the area's first vines.

Another early Hawke's Bay grape-grower was the prominent landowner and surveyor Henry Stokes Tiffen, who planted vines on some of his land at Taradale in 1857. He later sold two hectares to Bartholomew Steinmetz who, in 1901, began making wine labelled Taradale Vineyards. In the late 1920s, he hired a 14-year-old called Tom McDonald. Together this unlikely partnership formed the basis for what is the McDonald's Church Road Winery, owned today by Montana Wines. When McDonald was nearly 20, Steinmetz returned to his home country, Luxembourg, and his young protégé leased and then later purchased the winery from him. In the 1930s, McDonald was one of a trio of Bay winemakers producing fortified wines.

'Who says Hawke's Bay can't make bloody good pinot?' John Hancock, Trinity Hill winery

The others were Richard Ellis of Brookfields Vineyards and Robert Bird of Glenvale winery (now Esk Valley winery and owned by New Zealand's third largest winery, the Villa Maria Group).

Of these three producers, McDonald had the most significant impact on modern winemaking in New Zealand, but not in the form of fortified plonk. In 1949 he made New Zealand's first commercial cabernet sauvignon.

The first of the modern wave of wineries in Hawke's Bay to make a top-notch red was Te Mata Estate, started by John and Wendy Buck in 1978.

John describes his move from working as a wine merchant into making wine as a gradual evolution.

'I had seen a couple of quite smart wines from New Zealand when I was in England that people had sent over and when we came home, in 1966, we spent a day with Tom [McDonald] and tasted wines that showed top quality reds could be made in the region.'

Among the wines that impressed Buck were the 1965 McWilliam's Cabernet and a 1962 chardonnay.

'In both cases, the wines had good aromas that were true to the variety, which was not common in New Zealand at the time. I had come out of Europe and therefore my yardstick was European wines. There were qualities I looked for in wines and these two possessed the basic prerequisites,' says Buck.

And that, along with a wave of other new wineries started in the 1980s and 1990s in the Bay, started what has grown to become one of New Zealand's most dynamic and sophisticated wine regions.

In 1988, Montana Wines purchased McDonald's Church Road winery and turned it into an operation focused on producing premium and super-premium wines. In 1996, Montana released its priciest wine, called Tom, in honour of the region's most tenacious cabernet sauvignon pioneer. The wine Tom is a blend, predominantly of merlot and cabernet sauvignon.

Fruit salad or experimentation?

According to Tony Prichard, Hawke's Bay's regional winemaker for Montana Wines, 'We are very focused on merlot and cabernet sauvignon. We don't want to try to be all things to all people. It smacks of the fruit salad days of the past.'

However, others believe some experimentation is vital.

'I've got a really bad feeling that if we don't experiment then Hawke's Bay is going to be stuck in a terrible rut,' says winemaker John Hancock, of Trinity Hill winery.

The strongest thing Hawke's Bay has in its favour is diversity, says Hancock. The Bay, he says, has the possibility of making a huge range of different wines and wine styles.

He is testing out either an impressive or crazy number – depending on your perspective – of grape varieties that are new to the Hawke's Bay region.

When he is wearing his winemaker's hat, Hancock admits it could be problematic in the long term having 'too many different styles of wine in our portfolio', but when wearing his marketing hat, he says something entirely different.

'We would like to bat around the edge a little bit. If we can make the tempranillo grape work in Hawke's Bay, then we have a head start on everyone else.'

The same could be said for his experimental plantings and first wines made from the Italian grape montepulciano, and for pinot noir made from new experimental vineyards in the south of Hawke's Bay.

Hancock says he will let the market decide which wines it wants to drink before he makes fixed decisions on where the future will lead his winemaking.

The prerequisite for any new wines, he says, is their commercial acceptance in the marketplace.

'When we are looking at new grape varieties to fiddle with, we are probably looking at non-normal but still mainstream. I regard the tempranillo grape as a mainstream international variety.'

One thing that will change is his focus on cabernet sauvignon. Always known as a cabernet sauvignon and chardonnay fan, Hancock still favours these varieties over most others but says that, from 2004, syrah will begin to catch up with and then overtake cabernet sauvignon at Trinity Hill.

To make sure it is a distinctive style of wine, Hancock and fellow Trinity Hill winemaker Warren Gibson plan to add a small percentage of the white grape viognier to their syrah. It's standard practice in many Rhône wineries in France, and it changes the style of syrah from what Hancock describes as 'very masculine' into something 'very feminine'.

'The versatility of syrah is really quite amazing; adding viognier to syrah even in tiny quantities makes a dramatic difference to the taste of a wine.'

As far as the cabernet sauvignon versus merlot debate runs, Hancock sees the benefit in both, but says it is imperative to plant these grapes on the most suitable vineyard sites.

'Our top wines will remain dominated by cabernet sauvignon, and after 25 years of making wine here, the most important aspect of that is about finding the right soil to match with the right grape variety. I believe cabernet sauvignon is a particularly important case in point.

'I personally wouldn't consider growing cabernet sauvignon in any other soils or any other spot in the whole of New Zealand apart from the stoniest and warmest parts of Gimblett Gravels. It doesn't ripen consistently anywhere else … It would be very, very sad for cabernet sauvignon to become less important.'

At least there is something there for Te Mata Estate's Peter Cowley to agree with.

For many New Zealand red wine drinkers, Peter Cowley is Mr Cabernet Sauvignon. In 1985, Cowley went to Hawke's Bay to work at Te Mata Estate for owner John Buck. Experience at Lindemans in Coonawarra, Australia, and with Delegat's in Auckland, left Cowley with the lasting impression that the Bay possessed a climate far preferable to both of those locations.

'Hawke's Bay felt warmer than Coonawarra and drier than Auckland,' says the man who makes two of New Zealand's top wine offerings each year.

They are best known simply as Coleraine and Elston and these wines, a cabernet sauvignon-dominant blend and a chardonnay, do not come from grapes grown on the Gimblett Gravels.

As these wines consistently demonstrate, and as Cowley insists, there are other dependably warm microclimates in the Bay, perfectly suited to producing the relatively long-ripening cabernet sauvignon grape variety.

None of the experimental grapes in Hawke's Bay is new on a global scale but many are new to Hawke's Bay and to New Zealand. The reds include gamay noir, being pioneered in small quantities with

LEFT: Te Mata Peak overlooks the Tukituki River and Hawke's Bay, New Zealand's second biggest winemaking region.
BELOW: The famous Terraces vineyard at Esk Valley Estate, which is part of New Zealand's third biggest winery, the Villa Maria Group, owned by George Fistonich and based in Auckland.

high quality results, at both Te Mata and Te Awa Farm wineries. Montepulciano and tempranillo are being grown and turned into small quantities of wine at Trinity Hill. Zinfandel is being trialled at Kemblefield and petit verdot at Te Mata Estate.

Viognier is the most widely planted of the experimental white grapes and wineries testing the waters with this classic French variety include Babich Wines, Te Mata and Trinity Hill. It is early days but the region is producing slightly greenish tasting viognier.

Pinot gris has been grown for so long in the region that it has gone beyond being experimental but the quantities planted are tiny at under 40 hectares.

The wines made from pinot gris here, as in the rest of New Zealand, vary greatly in both style and quality.

Improved clones and rootstocks have been as important as the right climate and soils.

'It would be impossible for any experienced and good Hawke's Bay winemaker not to make better cabernet sauvignons and merlots than we did in the past,' says Montana's Church Road winemaker, Tony Prichard.

'We are all making better wines from these grapes than we used to because we did everything wrong in the past.

'The Bay's biggest strength is its ability to allow you to do an excellent job with most grape varieties in most years.'   Peter Cowley, Te Mata Estate

'We had the wrong clonal selections of these grapes, the wrong rootstocks on which they were grafted. We were growing grapes on the wrong vineyard sites and soils and we were inexperienced in making them.'

One of the greatest leaps forward has been the availability of improved clones. All of the grapes in Cowley's cabernet sauvignon-dominant blends today, for instance, are clones of Bordeaux grape varieties rather than those used in the past, many of which came from California.

'Our early experience makes us believe that the new clones may give us more concentration and complexity but the jury is still out on that,' says Cowley.

Rootstocks are another, more complex, issue. Chardonnay, cabernet sauvignon, merlot, syrah, pinot noir and riesling et al are all

LEFT ABOVE: Plunging the cap on The Terraces, Esk Valley's top red: (left to right) John Graham, Sean Beer and Gordon Russell.
BELOW FAR LEFT: Anna-Barbara and Bruce Helliwell's Unison Vineyard is home to some of Hawke's Bay's best reds made from cabernet sauvignon and merlot grapes.
BELOW LEFT: Riverview Vineyard, owned by medium-sized winery Morton Estate, which sources its grapes from Hawke's Bay and Marlborough but processes them currently at a Bay of Plenty-based winery in Tauranga.
ABOVE: Grapes at Unison Vineyard, a producer of top-notch red wines.

varieties of the species of grapevine known as *Vitis vinifera*. It is the most important vine from which to make wine but it is prone to a vine-eating louse called phylloxera. To prevent phylloxera, *Vitis vinifera* vines are grafted onto phylloxera-resistant rootstock. Many of the other members of the *Vitis* species are phylloxera resistant but also have other desirable or undesirable characters, like the ability to either promote or devigorate the growth of the vine that is grafted on to them.

'We now use a mix of less vigorous rootstock, wherever it is appropriate,' says Cowley. 'But it will take another 20 years to find the perfect rootstock for the right soils and grape varieties.'

The queen of the wine world, chardonnay, is the most planted grape in Hawke's Bay. In 2002, there were 957 hectares of the variety planted in the region, making it second to Marlborough.

Until recently, many of the region's winemakers have not viewed chardonnay as much of a challenge. Montana's Tony Prichard says: 'Chardonnay is not as challenging to make as the reds.' He adds quickly, however, that chardonnay is of massive importance to the Hawke's Bay wine industry, not only as a bread and butter wine grape variety but because it contributes significantly to the region's image as a quality wine producing area.

'We realise now that chardonnay is more sensitive than we had initially thought and in order to harness the best from it we need to be vigilant in the vineyard.'

Tony Prichard, Church Road

More recently he has revised his stance.

It has become a cliché in the wine industry these days but the fact is that wine is, first and foremost, made in the vineyard. Without good grapes, no winemaker can put a decent taste of anything in a bottle. Not only are New Zealand winemakers and grape-growers more interested in harnessing the best flavours from their vineyards, like Tony Prichard, they are now more adept at seeing the nuances of what happens there.

Not that the chardonnays Prichard has made so far have been under par. Far from it. For the vast number of New Zealand wine drinkers, Church Road Chardonnay is one of their stand-by dinner party wines but, in his quest to make better wines, Prichard is now de-emphasising the very thing that has always characterised most of

ABOVE: Winemaker Tony Prichard at Church Road winery is part of an innovative team at the giant Montana Wines Hawke's Bay operation.
RIGHT: The cellar at Esk Valley winery in Bay View, just north of Napier city.
FAR RIGHT: Esk Valley winemaker looking at grapes.

'I know the world is full of chardonnay, but Hawke's Bay's versions seems to me to be an amalgam of the ripe fruits found in Gisborne wines with a more steely grapefruit nuance found in the more southern New Zealand chardonnays.'

Gordon Russell, Esk Valley winemaker

this country's chardonnays: their overtly vibrant fruit tastes and the impression of sweetness.

'We are looking for something other than single dimensional fruit flavours but which sits on the basis of clean, ripe fruit,' explains the winemaker. He is gaining the subtle and satisfying extras in his chardonnay today by harvesting the grapes earlier than in the past, leaving the wine longer on its yeast lees and stirring the lees more than previously too. Most importantly, Prichard hopes, the result will be a wine that will age better than before. Along with the Church Road Reserve Chardonnay is the experimental Cuve Series Chardonnay, which sells only at the winery cellar door, and is his most exciting, subtle, clean and silky chardonnay.

'We are trying to set both wines up for a very slow and graceful development in the bottle. We want to create chardonnays that are more able to develop complexities of taste once bottled.'

Prichard is not the only one in the Bay to see chardonnay as its greatest white hope. Gordon Russell, winemaker at Esk Valley, says the best chardonnays in the region have the ability to age and gain considerable complexity.

For chardonnay, clonal diversity is important for winemakers, both from a quality and from a business perspective, says Vidal Estate winemaker, Rod McDonald.

'There are huge differences in the crop levels and flavours of the chardonnay clones available.

'Chardonnay clones that crop at relatively low levels are often considered superior for premium wines but are not economically viable for lower priced wines. So most wineries in the Bay today have a mix of chardonnay clones from which to choose to make wines across all price levels.'

It has been a hard climb up from virused clones because, for most winemakers, the sheer availability of good quality chardonnay grape clones has been a tricky hurdle to overcome.

The new wave of Hawke's Bay chardonnays is less reliant on the taste of oak barrels taken up during malolactic fermentation (a secondary fermentation in a wine that converts relatively hard malic acids in grapes to softer lactic ones). Instead and because of the new clones of chardonnay available today, the taste of the chardonnay grape itself is allowed to shine.

Some chardonnay grown in the Bay is also used to make sparkling wine.

Kate Radburnd of C.J. Pask winery says, 'Just for fun we make small volumes of sparkling wine from chardonnay and pinot noir.'

Another aspect new to chardonnay in the Bay is blending it with other dry white grape varieties, like viognier and roussanne.

'I think we will start seeing people look at chardonnay and other grapes blended together. They will not be large volume things but will extend the chardonnay theme a little bit, adding an exciting new taste,' says Steve Smith, of Craggy Range winery.

Sauvignon blanc lurks in the shadows of Hawke's Bay's white grape vineyards. It is the region's fourth most planted grape variety but probably is its most under-appreciated.

Few winemakers bother to talk about this grape variety but those who warrant it worth a mention clearly see sauvignon blanc as a valid alternative to chardonnay and to the relatively more dramatic, powerful and pack-a-punch sauvignon blancs made in Marlborough.

By contrast, Hawke's Bay sauvignon blanc is stylistically softer and more texturally driven than the pungently distinctive wines from Marlborough, which tend to be more in your face.

The future of the tried and true grapes, chardonnay and merlot, is what Kate Radburnd is most excited about and she acknowledges that syrah will become hugely significant in the Bay.

As chief winemaker and part-owner of C.J. Pask wines, Radburnd has seen dramatic changes in Hawke's Bay over the last 20 years. As the vineyards get older and winemakers' understanding improves, Radburnd sees great things for chardonnay, merlot and syrah.

ABOVE: Neat rows of vines in the Esk Valley, an area cooled by sea breezes.

Hawke's Bay wineries

Akarangi Wines

River Road, Hawke's Bay, phone (06) 877 8228

Alpha Domus

1829 Maraekakaho Road, Bridge Pa, Hawke's Bay, phone (06) 879 6752

Askerne Vineyard

267 Te Mata-Mangateretere Road, Havelock North, phone (06) 877 6085

Bilancia

State Highway 50, Hastings, phone (06) 879 9711

Bradshaw Estate Winery

295 Te Mata Road, RD 12, Havelock North, phone (06) 877 5795

Brookfields Vineyard

376 Brookfields Road, Meeanee, Hawke's Bay, phone (06) 834 4615

C.J. Pask Winery

1133 Omahu Road, Hastings, phone (06) 879 7906

Central Hawke's Bay Wine Company

RD 2, Takapau, Hawke's Bay, phone (06) 855 8318

Church Road Winery

200 Church Road, Taradale, Napier, phone (06) 844 2053

Clearview Estate Winery

Clifton Road, Te Awanga, Hawke's Bay, phone (06) 875 0150

Crab Farm Winery

511 Main Road, Bay View, Hawke's Bay, phone (06) 836 6678

Craggy Range Vineyard

252 Waimarama Road, Havelock North, phone (06) 877 7126

Crossroads Winery

Korokipo Road, Fernhill, Napier, phone (06) 879 9737

Equinox Wines

154 Moteo Pa Road, RD 3, Napier, phone (06) 844 9804

Esk Valley Estate

745 Main Road North, Bay View, Napier, phone (06) 836 6411

Hatton Estate Gimblett Road

12 Palmerston Road, Havelock North, phone (06) 877 7693

Huthlee Estate Vineyard

84 Montana Road, RD 5, Hastings, phone (06) 879 6234

Kemblefield Estate Winery

Aorangi Road, Mangatahi, Hawke's Bay, phone (06) 874 9649

Kim Crawford Wines

Clifton Road, Te Awanga, Hawke's Bay, phone (09) 529 0804

Linden Estate

347 State Highway 5, Esk Valley, RD 2, Napier, phone (06) 836 6806

Lombardi Wines

Te Mata Road, Havelock North, phone (06) 877 7985

Lucknow Estate Winery

3764 State Highway 50, RD 1, Maraekakaho, Hawke's Bay, phone (06) 874 9007

Matariki Wines

52 Kirkwood Road, Hastings, phone (06) 879 6226

Mission Estate Winery

198 Church Road, Taradale, Napier, phone (06) 844 2259

Ngatarawa Wines

Ngatarawa Road, RD 5, Hastings, phone (06) 879 7603

Park Estate Winery

2087 Pakowhai Road, RD 3, Napier, phone (06) 844 8137

Prospect Vineyard

1950 Maraekakaho Road, RD 1, Hastings, phone (06) 879 5686

Redmetal Vineyards

Maraekakaho Road, Bridge Pa, Hawke's Bay, phone (06) 879 6567

Riverside Wines New Zealand

Dartmoor Road, Puketapu, Napier, phone (06) 844 4942

Sacred Hill Wines

1033 Dartmoor Road, Puketapu, Napier, phone (06) 879 8760

Sileni Estates

2016 Maraekakaho Road, Bridge Pa, Napier, phone (06) 879 8768

Stonecroft Wines

121 Mere Road, Hastings, phone (06) 879 9610

Te Awa Farm Winery

2375 State Highway 50, RD 5, Hastings, phone (06) 879 7602

Te Mata Estate Winery

349 Te Mata Road, Havelock North, phone (06) 877 4399

Trinity Hill

2396 State Highway 50, Roys Hill, Hawke's Bay, phone (06) 879 7778

Unison Vineyard

2163 State Highway 50, Hastings, phone (06) 879 7913

Vidal Estate

913 St Aubyn Street East, Hastings, phone (06) 876 9662

Wairarapa

Martinborough is the heart of the Wairarapa wine scene. Its transformation from once-dull east coast country town to buzzing, chic and stylish destination is nothing short of breathtaking. A travel guide once advised passers-through Martinborough to keep on going since it was the sort of place where you might be lucky to find an open fish and chip shop. Now its boredom has been banished and the dowdy town has been transformed as historic buildings have been trucked in, renovated and opened for business as wine bars, food stores and restaurants. The winemakers here grow a wide range of grapes from cabernets franc and sauvignon to pinot noir and syrah, as well as a long list of whites.

Larry McKenna is a busy man. For a start he is pioneering a whole new winery, which means his attentions are divided between the rigmarole of paperwork and the excitement of planting vast new vineyards in a new sub-region of Martinborough.

Then he has to make the wines and, hardest of all, market them, find a point of difference in the way he does that and create wines that are unique enough to start selling themselves.

McKenna is one of a partnership that includes four people in the relatively new Escarpment Vineyard, situated on Te Muna Road, west of the Martinborough township.

Of the 24 hectares of vines he had planted at the time of writing, 70 percent were pinot noir, with the remainder being chardonnay, riesling, sauvignon blanc, pinot gris and pinot blanc.

It was easy to stay in Martinborough for his next project, although it was tempting to go home to a good offer in Victoria, Australia. The opportunity to buy land in Martinborough and capitalise on what he had achieved outweighed the advantage of starting somewhere else.

'Call this region what you will but in terms of soils it is the same as the vineyards around Martinborough and the climate is similar too.'

The difference is the diurnal range at Te Muna is bigger than it is for vineyards planted around the Martinborough township.

Te Muna is hotter in summer and cooler in winter with a slightly higher risk of frosts, according to McKenna.

PREVIOUS PAGES: Craggy Range Vineyards' vast new plantings of pinot noir and sauvignon blanc on Martinborough's Te Muna Terraces are owned by Australian businessman Terry Peabody and New Zealand viticulturist and Master of Wine Steve Smith, and their respective families.
ABOVE: Despite a plethora of international wine awards, the machinery is never idle for long at the famous Ata Rangi winery, on Puruatanga Road, Martinborough.
RIGHT: Grape-growers and winemakers endeavour to match the trellising system to the requirements of the grape variety and local climatic conditions, in order to harness the best flavours from their grapes.

If McKenna is busy then one of the owners of Te Muna's other vast new vineyard, Master of Wine Steve Smith, is frantic.

Smith is one of New Zealand's most experienced viticulturists, a partner and general manager in the Hawke's Bay-based winery, Craggy Range. His enthusiasm for Martinborough sauvignon blanc and pinot noir is as great as his passion for the soils and rocks on which they are grown.

'Martinborough was the obvious place for us to grow pinot noir because the country's best and most consistently good pinot noirs come out of this region,' says Smith, of the new double-terraced vineyards he has overseen the planting of at Te Muna.

Martinborough is also relatively close to Hawke's Bay, where the Craggy Range winery is based, so transporting grapes from one region to the next becomes less problematic than if the distance were greater, as is usually the case anywhere else in New Zealand.

Craggy Range winery makes two distinctive sauvignon blancs from Marlborough and to add to that stable of aromatic whites, Smith has a significant number of sauvignon blanc vines planted in Martinborough, alongside pinot noir, chardonnay and riesling.

'The quality of Martinborough sauvignon blanc is uniformly high, which was the main drawcard for us to come here   that and the slightly riper, more tropical spectrum of flavour derived from sauvignon blanc grapes grown in Martinborough.'

Until recently the Wairarapa was a tiny wine region in terms of production, even by New Zealand's standards. However, its importance has never been in question. Quite the opposite.

Wairarapa's winemakers are generally characterised by their quest for perfection. This has been possible for two reasons, the first of which relates to the region's benevolent grape-growing climate. 'The climate here errs on the cool side but the summer is long enough and warm enough to allow a wide range of grapes with different needs to all ripen well,' explains Dry River's Neil McCallum.

Secondly, the amounts of wine produced by most wineries here are small enough to allow their makers to focus on quality, beginning in the vineyard with vigorous pruning regimes and green harvesting – dropping a percentage of grapes on the ground. The grapes left are more concentrated in flavour as a result of being reduced in number.

The coolest and driest of the North Island's winemaking regions, Wairarapa has relatively low rainfall, warm to hot days and cool nights – conditions which combine to create an environment in which grapes can slowly ripen, particularly in autumn. These climatic conditions, coupled with free-draining soils, many based on old river terraces, create a highly desirable place in which to grow pinot noir, sauvignon blanc and riesling, all of which benefit from developing flavours slowly. These conditions also allow the early ripening chardonnay and relatively late ripening cabernet sauvignon and merlot to grow with ease in this region, but the wines made from these grapes are noticeably affected by vintage variations, in terms of the flavours in the resulting wines.

Bounded by the Rimutaka and Tararua ranges on the west and rolling hills near the coast in the east, the economy of the Wairarapa plains was built on the back of sheep, with farms being established in the 1850s.

The region is often referred to as Wellington, a reference to a small vineyard planted on the Kapiti Coast, at Te Horo, nearly an hour's drive north of Wellington city. This area is away from the winds that buffet the 'Windy City' and the climate is warmer and wetter.

As a grape-growing and winemaking region, the Wairarapa has a name and reputation that far outweighs its size. Tiny vineyards typify the Wairarapa, with a low average output from each, but this is changing slowly as medium and large wineries establish themselves and their vineyards in the area.

To date, however, the region contributes just four percent to New Zealand's total annual wine production and even with massive new vineyards planted, this percentage is not anticipated to change by 2005 because the country's entire national vineyard is growing fast.

The Wairarapa's biggest advantage lies in having 350,000 people living over the Rimutaka Ranges in Wellington city: a large fan base on which to try out their first and subsequent wines.

The first grapes known to be planted in the Wairarapa were in 1883 by landowner and farmer William Beetham, who had a vineyard in the north near Masterton. Vines then disappeared from the region, when the threat of national prohibition gripped the country at the turn of the twentieth century.

Wairarapa's modern day wine scene began in the late 1970s when publisher Alister Taylor planted white grapes on land that later became Te Kairanga winery. At the same time, soil scientist Dr Derek Milne noted in a report, in 1979, that Martinborough's climate would favour grape-growing for winemaking. Then the action started.

LEFT: Few people are as well-acquainted with the ups and downs of winemaking in Martinborough as Larry McKenna of the relatively new Escarpment Vineyard. He is one of the most experienced winemakers in the Wairarapa, having worked at Martinborough Vineyard from 1986 to 1999, initially as winemaker and then as general manager, before moving on to his own new project at the turn of the millennium.
BELOW: There is a fruit salad of grape varieties grown in the Wairarapa's vineyards because, like its northern cousin, the Hawke's Bay, this region has extremely versatile growing conditions that suit a wide range of different grapes.

Milne co-founded Martinborough Vineyard with five others, in 1980. Dr Neil McCallum of Dry River Wines had planted grapes in 1979, Clive Paton of Ata Rangi planted grapes in 1980 and Stan Chifney had the region's first working winery, established in 1983. They are not only the oldest wineries in the modern Wairarapa wine scene but also the most highly regarded.

The number of wineries in Martinborough has grown hugely since the mid-1980s, jumping from 18 in the 'Wellington' region to 45 in 2002. Areas surrounding Martinborough are also being planted with grapes.

The closest to Martinborough is the relatively new Te Muna Road area, about five kilometres west of the township as the crow flies and about nine kilometres' drive. Further south, on the banks of the Huangarua River, there is a smattering of new vineyards, including Palliser Estate winemaker Allan Johnson's new plantings. This area is called Ruakokoputuna, a green, lush area that is, confesses Johnson, a little wetter than around Martinborough.

For years the northern Wairarapa winery, Solstone, near Masterton township, and the Gladstone Vineyard near Carterton were the region's only non-Martinborough wineries. Now there are adventurous grape-growers and winemakers scattered all through the Wairarapa basin.

The most significant and extensive new plantings outside the confines of Martinborough are in an area called Dakin's Road, also known as East Taratahi and the Wairarapa Valley. Hundreds of hectares of relatively new grapevines were planted here in the late 1990s and are beginning to produce a wide range of wines, including sauvignon blanc, pinot noirs and a smattering of cabernet sauvignon, merlot and malbec.

'The jury is out on what this area will grow best, so we are trying a wide range,' said winemaker Paddy Borthwick of Borthwick Estate, around the turn of the millennium.

Mention New Zealand red wine to anyone who drinks it and lives outside New Zealand and the words that are most likely to spring to their lips are 'pinot noir'.

And now that pinot noir vineyards are spreading like wildfire through the country, New Zealand's reputation for top quality pinot noir is being rapidly cemented. It was the consistently high quality of wines made in Martinborough that led this country's wine industry into pinot fever.

The Wairarapa's most successful wineries are those run by winemakers who own them, says Dr Neil McCallum from Dry River Wines.

ABOVE: Even busy winemakers relax occasionally. Roger Parkinson owns and operates Nga Waka Vineyard, one of the oldest and smallest wineries in Martinborough. Parkinson planted his first grapes there in 1988.
RIGHT: Architect Max Herriott broke new ground when he designed Nga Waka winery, which is built in Coloursteel and concrete blocks. Plantings around this modern design are entirely native species.

At the time of writing, McCallum had joined the growing number of New Zealand winemakers who have sold their wineries and vineyards to overseas concerns but he remained adamant that he would stay at the winemaking helm – 'At least for the foreseeable future,' he added, sagely.

'The key to what makes the best wineries in Martinborough are the winemakers who have their finger on the pulse.'

McCallum sold because he found it to be too frantic coping with the paperwork that goes with running a small business.

Now that he is able to concentrate on what really matters, McCallum sees the brightest future in the region for pinot noir but he also makes some of the best riesling and pinot gris in New Zealand each year and another red variety that has him stunned: syrah.

In 2003 syrah occupied just four percent of the region's vineyard.

'I find it extraordinary that our syrah gets so much acceptance,' says Neil McCallum.

'People get really excited about it, including the Australians whose shiraz (the same grape, under different nomenclature) is entirely at odds with our style.'

The same is true of Martinborough's other most famous big name but small production winery, Ata Rangi, where the owners, who are also the viticulturists and winemakers, fashion what is fast emerging to be one of New Zealand's best tasting syrahs.

The irony is that Ata Rangi is widely considered globally to be New Zealand's most consistent producer of pinot noir. Its success with syrah is accidental rather than by design, since the winery's focus has been primarily on producing top quality pinot noir.

By adhering to the same quality driven philosophy behind the strict Ata Rangi regime in the vineyard (low yields being paramount in this), the team here has succeeded in making a silky syrah that is one of the best in New Zealand. The 2002 Ata Rangi Syrah, one of the few wines to be mentioned specifically in this book, is noteworthy because it is sealed with a screw cap. Contentious as this wine seal is, for the team at Ata Rangi – and many other New Zealand wineries – it is the obvious way to move forward.

Winemaker Oliver Masters says the overriding consideration for him and others at Ata Rangi is that most people who buy their wines will be drinking them within the first two or three years of purchase.

'For those who cellar the wines longer they will find the wine in better condition as a result of the screw cap. How the development profile will compare is hard to quantify but the end result, whatever the time span, is going to be more satisfying to a larger number of people as a result of the screw cap seal,' says Masters.

'As a result of spending too much good money on bad bottles of wine, from all over the world, we are so far certainly enjoying our decision to go with screw caps.'

(In 2003, it was expected that some 20 percent of New Zealand wines would be sealed with screw caps by the start of 2004, and this percentage was predicted to increase.)

For Dry River's Neil McCallum the decision to stay with cork seals for now is also based on quality. He focuses strongly on sourcing the best quality cork he can as well as waiting for evidence to mount that can indicate how red wines will fare under other seals, especially in the long term.

'We don't have that evidence yet and my wines are not made for immediate consumption,' explains the winemaker.

McCallum's wide ranging focus on different wines and styles plays to the region's versatile climate. He grows a variety of grapes that ripen at varying times throughout late summer and autumn.

'The Wairarapa is close to the coast on both the south and east sides but the climate tends to be relatively dry, a factor that is enhanced by vigorous spring and summer winds. Although these winds often wipe out entire crops of the sensitive gewürztraminer grape and make everything more tricky for pinot noir.

'Most of the comments we get about our syrah comes down to people thinking that it comes straight out of the Rhône Valley, France. They are amazed to find it is from New Zealand and a relatively cool area of the country at that.' Dr Neil McCallum, Dry River Wines

'Martinborough's strength is the variety of wines and styles it can produce at a strong level, ranging from cool climate gewürztraminer and pinot gris right up to syrah.'

Vine age or better clones? It's a question that vexes winemakers in New Zealand, where everything about the country's wine industry is relatively young.

When Ata Rangi winery's other winemaker, Clive Paton, had made 12 vintages of wine at the turn of the new millennium, he added another factor into the quality equation: winemaker age.

'If I had the last 10 years all over again I would know how to do everything better and I expect to see significant improvement in our wines over the next decade because of winemaker age,' said Paton.

BELOW FAR LEFT: Time rarely stands still in New Zealand's fast-growing wine scene. Ata Rangi's former assistant winemaker, Grant Stanley, was head-hunted by Quails Gate in Okanagan, British Columbia.
BELOW LEFT: Winemaker Grant Stanley extracts Ata Rangi winery's unfinished pinot noir into tasting glasses.
BELOW: A rare moment in his favourite chair. Lawyer-turned-winemaker John Porter insists that he hardly ever gets the chance to put his feet up between to-ing and fro-ing from Wellington, where he still works part-time as a lawyer, and Martinborough, where he and his family now live and produce tiny quantities of top-notch pinot gris and pinot noir.

'You can clearly taste whatever has been done to pinot noir, either in the vineyard or in the winery whereas with other varieties it is not so obvious. The more you understand that principle, and the more seasons you have under your belt, then the more licence you have to get the best from pinot.' Clive Paton, Ata Rangi

'Pinot noir is more seasonally variable than most other varieties. If you look at the warm end of the climate spectrum, then in a year like 1998 the wines will be hugely different compared with wines from a cooler year, which could be, say, 2000.'

Taking 1998 as an example, Paton says that the region's most established winemakers will have an edge as their vines gain age over the next decade, purely because of the experience that wildcard vintages like this throw at them.

'The 1998 vintage was my biggest learning curve to date. We ended up making wines that were more like syrah than pinot noir and because we have experienced a vintage like that we know not to do so much extraction in the winery, not just in a hot year but also in a cool year because it will then accentuate any green flavours.'

Clive Paton and the other winemakers at Ata Rangi, Phyll Pattie and Oliver Masters, are aiming to create a pinot noir over the next decade that has more layers of fruit flavour and complexity. 'We want to add structure so it has more length of flavour and concentration of the flavour of pinot noir in the middle of the palate.'

Few wines present more of a challenge to winemakers than pinot noir. It is tricky to grow because it is more sensitive than most other grape varieties to frost and wind.

'Like Nelson and Waipara and Central Otago, Martinborough has been a place full of experimentation and success with a small band of early winemakers defining the success of the entire region.' Philip Gregan, CEO Winegrowers New Zealand

In Master of Wine Jancis Robinson's *Guide to Wine Grapes*, she says: 'Pinot noir has for long been grown in Burgundy (France) but it is particularly prone to mutate.'

None of this appears to be a deterrent to winemakers around the world and in New Zealand, in particular, where pinot noir is the most planted red grape variety today. The most consistent quality pinot noirs in the country have to date been made in Martinborough.

Experimentation gave others new to the region and around the country the idea that New Zealand can make top quality pinot noir, but that doesn't mean winemakers can rest on their laurels, says Martinborough winemaker Larry McKenna.

The biggest challenge for winemakers in the Wairarapa today, he says, is to broaden the definition of what the ultimate pinot noir is.

'We have to expand the style in order to succeed with it because now we are at the stage where New Zealand pinot noir is almost like sauvignon blanc. You know what it's going to taste like before you even open the bottle. We have to get more adventurous in terms of styles we make.'

Pinot noir is the region's most widely planted grape, making up 62 percent of the area's total vineyard area in 2003, but high quality wines are also consistently made here from sauvignon blanc, chardonnay, riesling, cabernet sauvignon and pinot gris.

The region's biggest winery is Palliser Estate, which was established in 1984 and hit its stride immediately as a top notch producer of chardonnay, riesling and sauvignon blanc.

Palliser Estate's white wines are consistently among the best in the country and in 1996 its pinot noir turned the corner from being a good wine to being exceptionally good, as a vertical tasting of older vintages demonstrated to wine writers in 2001.

The biggest change for the winery was in lowering the cropping level, the level of grapes that it took from each vine. Even so, the 1999 and 2000 wines were the best, showing a rise in quality and evolution towards more complex wines.

Winemaker Allan Johnson has his own small vineyard, planted in the late 1990s, east and slightly south of Martinborough township near the old Ruakokoputuna town. Here, he plans to pioneer the region's most southern pinot noir to date, when he makes the first wine some time this decade. Quantities will be tiny and the quality and style will not compete with Palliser Estate, he says, because it will be a different stylistic interpretation of pinot noir.

'The climate at Ruakokoputuna will see to that.'

Like most of the region's, and country's, pinot noir producers, Johnson is busily planting new-to-New-Zealand Dijon clones when the opportunities in the vineyard arise. 'They are most likely to have a very beneficial impact on the style and quality of our wines,' he says, 'but more than anything they open up the options for the styles of pinot noir we make.'

The other red grape that has a staunchly loyal following in this region is cabernet sauvignon.

It was first planted in the early 1980s by Stan Chifney, whose winery and vineyard were sold to Margrain winery in 2001.

Bill Benfield and Sue Delamare at Benfield & Delamare planted cabernet in 1987.

'The region hadn't really settled down with any particular grape variety back then,' explains Benfield, adding that things could have gone either way when he and Delamare were taken under Stan Chifney's wing and got the cabernet bug.

Today they have two hectares planted in cabernet sauvignon, cabernet franc and merlot. Merlot is the predominant grape and it is planted on the heavier soils in the region. They do not buy in grapes because they are focused on top quality, insists Benfield. 'We rigidly control our vineyards and have found when we looked at buying in fruit in the past, it just wasn't up to scratch.'

They have set up their vineyard to focus on ripening their chosen grape varieties as efficiently as possible, including stringently chosen rootstocks that their grapes are grafted onto, the spacing of their vine rows, even the height of their trellis.

LEFT: Allan Johnson, winemaker at Palliser Estate, is one of the Wairarapa's most experienced winemakers. Like many in the region he found his own piece of land, moved a house there and planted this vineyard, south of Martinborough township.
ABOVE: Craggy Range Vineyards' Martinborough viticulturist Peter Wilkins.

It is the region's relatively long season that Benfield points to, rather than the notion that the area is cool.

'If you look at heat summation days, then we are slightly warmer than Bordeaux, so heat is not a problem.'

At just 200 cases of annual wine production, Benfield & Delamare is one of the region's tiniest wineries. The second aspect to their business is the breeding of rootstocks, which they sell to other wineries and vineyards.

When he first planted grapes in the Dakin's Road area of the Wairarapa, winemaker Paddy Borthwick said cabernet sauvignon was fine in good years but he wanted to focus more on the pinot market and burgundy varieties rather than Bordeaux varieties.

The aim is to find more consistency within that long season. 'In a good year the cabernets are very good but when it's not that warm then the cabernet is not that great and we have had years when we don't even pick it.'

In 2002 Borthwick pulled out all of his cabernet sauvignon vines. He now has 18 hectares and a new winery. He plans to plant another nine hectares, predominantly in pinot noir followed by sauvignon blanc, chardonnay and riesling.

Sauvignon blanc is the region's most planted white grape. In taste it is stylistically similar to Marlborough sauvignon blanc, with more body. Chardonnay is the region's next biggest grape, with a hefty 67 hectares planted and a strong, bold style of wine made from it. Riesling, pinot gris and gewürztraminer made in this region are among the best in New Zealand.

Martinborough Vineyard winemaker Claire Mulholland moved here from Central Otago in 2000, excited to work with and challenged by the 10 different pinot noir clones that are grown on the winery's vineyards. 'It's a wider selection than I had previously worked with and there was a noticeable difference in rate of flavour development and tannin maturity in Martinborough, compared to down south.'

Like most winemakers in the region, she sees pinot noir as the big hope for the future with chardonnay as next in line.

'The biggest improvement we can make in both pinot noir and chardonnay in this region is by trialling new clones of both grapes in order to harness the best from them and to continue learning about what works best.'

At a 10-year retrospective tasting, held in 2001, it was not chardonnay but rather riesling that held its own over the long haul. The most exciting riesling came from the tiny Nga Waka Vineyard, owned by winemaker Roger Parkinson.

ABOVE: In the 25 years since Martinborough Vineyard began, it has had just two winemakers. Claire Mulholland, who moved from Central Otago to the Wairarapa in 2000, is the second of these, pictured here under old pinot noir vines surrounding the winery and cellar door.
RIGHT: On their way to one of the region's winemakers' gatherings are Annabel Clayton of Porter's Pinot, with her and John Porter's children (left to right): Millie, Hugo (in front), Zoe (tucked in behind Hugo), Annabel (mum), Imogen, a friend, Louise, and the family dog, Lucy.

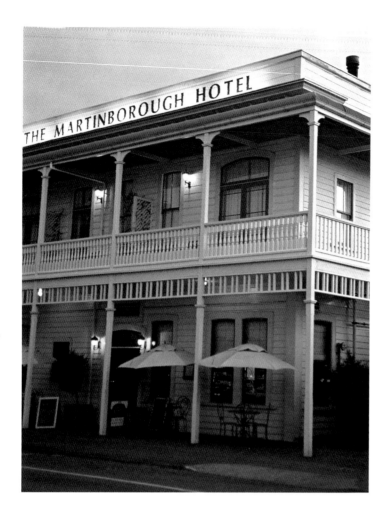

Like many winemakers in the region, he hand-picks all of his grapes, treating them to the gentlest of processing by whole-bunch pressing, following which he goes down the pricey route of ageing his rieslings for a year in the bottle before selling them.

'This way it gives the wine time to evolve from a steely young creature into a wine that is more approachable in flavour,' says this quietly spoken perfectionist.

The Wairarapa's northernmost winery, Solstone Estate has its focus largely on Bordeaux red grape varieties with a smattering of pinot noir, sauvignon blanc and chardonnay. It is home to some of the region's oldest grapevines, dating back to 1981. In 2003, a new winemaker called Bernard Newman arrived fresh off the boat from working in Australia's Hunter Valley, keen to develop the white grape, sémillon.

'We have a Bordeaux focus here on red grapes, with cabernet sauvignon, cabernet franc and merlot but I am excited about the potential of sémillon because it fits in perfectly with the continuing education of New Zealand wine drinkers, who are becoming more interested in the idea of ageing and cellaring wine, as well as being able to drink new and interesting whites.'

To date, most of the vineyards in the Wairarapa have tended to be planted in the east, away from the rainfall predominant in the west. Newman sees the western Wairarapa and, possibly, slightly further north than the confines of the Wairarapa as areas worth exploring for sémillon.

'If we plant sémillon in the rain shadow at Opaki, for instance, it might just suit that grape really well in terms of getting it away from the drought stress that assists with the growing of other grapes.'

Climatic conditions in the west, he says, are very similar to the growing conditions in the Hunter Valley in Australia, where rain is a major factor that comes into play and, in a roundabout way, plays a role in producing top quality, long lived sémillons.

Small quantities of consistently high quality wine over the last two decades have helped the region's wineries to establish and cement a reputation that has put many of them at the forefront of New Zealand's wine production.

Most notable are Dry River, Ata Rangi, Martinborough Vineyard, Te Kairanga, Voss Estate, Walnut Ridge (now owned by Ata Rangi), Murdoch James, Margrain Vineyard and Gladstone Vineyard. These and other wineries have carved out a niche in the New Zealand and international markets for quality Wairarapa wine.

ABOVE: The Martinborough Hotel. Less than a decade ago, this place was, like many old hotels in New Zealand's North Island, run down, boarded up and closed for business. Now its bar and restaurant are booming and there is usually a waiting list to stay in the plush refurbished rooms.
RIGHT: Cape Palliser on the wild and windy Wairarapa south coast is home to numerous seal colonies.

Wairarapa wineries

Alana Estate

Puruatanga Road, Martinborough, phone (06) 306 9784

Alexander Vineyard Martinborough

Dublin Street Extension, Martinborough, phone (06) 306 8171

Ashwell Vineyards

Kitchener Street, Martinborough, phone (04) 472 0519

Ata Rangi

Puruatanga Road, Martinborough, phone (06) 306 9570

Benfield & Delamare

35 New York Street, Martinborough, phone (06) 306 9926

Borthwick Vineyard

Te Kopi Road, RD 4, Gladstone, Masterton, phone (06) 372 7512

Burnt Spur Martinborough

Kitchener Street, Martinborough, phone (06) 306 9174

Canadoro Wines

New York Street, Martinborough, phone (06) 306 8801

Cirrus Estate

Regent Street, Martinborough, phone 025 735 604

Claddagh Vineyard

Phone (06) 306 9264

Coney Wines

Dry River Road, Martinborough, phone (06) 306 8345

Dry River Wines

Puruatanga Road, Martinborough, phone (06) 306 9388

Escarpment Vineyard, The

Te Muna Road, Martinborough, phone (06) 306 9301

Fairmont Estate Winery

Gladstone Road, RD 2, Wairarapa, phone (06) 379 8498.

Gladstone Vineyard

Gladstone Road, RD 2, Carterton, phone (06) 379 8563

Hau Ariki Wines

Phone (06) 306 9360

Margrain Vineyard

Cnr Ponatahi and Huangarua Roads, Martinborough, phone (06) 306 9202

Martinborough Vineyard

Princess Street, Martinborough, phone (06) 306 9955

Mebus Estate

Dakins Road, RD 7, Masterton, phone (06) 377 3696

Muirlea Rise

Princess Street, Martinborough, phone (06) 306 8510

Murdoch James Estate

Dry River Road, Martinborough, phone (06) 306 9165

Nga Waka Vineyard

Kitchener Street, Martinborough, phone (06) 306 9832

Palliser Estate Wines of Martinborough

Kitchener Street, Martinborough, phone (06) 306 9019

Porter's Pinot

Kitchener Street, Martinborough, phone (06) 306 9013

Solstone Estate Winery

Solway Crescent, Masterton, phone (06) 377 5505

Stratford Wines

New York Street, Martinborough, phone (06) 306 9257

Te Horo Vineyards

Lucky SF, Main Road South, RD 1, Otaki, phone (06) 364 3392

Te Kairanga Wines

Martins Road, Martinborough, phone (06) 306 9122

Voss Estate Vineyards

Puruatanga Road, Martinborough, phone (06) 306 9668

Winslow Wines

Princess Street, Martinborough, phone (06) 306 9648

Nelson

Nelson winemakers are on the verge of discovering a strong identity for their wines, after decades of lurking in the shadow of their vinous neighbour, Marlborough. Until this century, many Nelson winemakers bought in grapes from Marlborough but now, spurred on by its best small winemakers, the region's biggest producers have decided to go it alone. Vast new vineyards, foreign investment and local wine knowledge mean Nelson can finally bask in the rays of its own plentiful sunshine.

It is a spring day in Nelson like any other, blissfully sunny and surprisingly relaxed, as I fly into this small city on the seaside in Tasman Bay in the north of the South Island. At Neudorf Vineyards, in an idyllic setting in the Upper Moutere Hills, the staff are enjoying the full force of the sun's warmth and the coolness of one of its best wines. And one of the region's best winemakers, Tim Finn, is pleased with his just-bottled, soft-textured, incredibly fresh 2003 Neudorf Nelson Sauvignon Blanc, sealed with a screw cap.

'We have been looking at one style of chardonnay and now we are going to have to find a whole new way of looking at the variety, because of the different expressions of the grapes we are getting.' Tim Finn, Neudorf Vineyards

PREVIOUS PAGES: Neudorf Vineyards, nestled in the picture-perfect Upper Moutere area of Nelson, is one of the region's oldest wineries and vineyards as well as its best known, high-quality producer.
ABOVE: Tim Finn, a former dairying advisory officer, named Neudorf Vineyards in homage to the German settlers who, briefly, came to Nelson in the nineteenth century to plant grapes.
RIGHT: John Kavanagh, winemaker at Neudorf Vineyards, strolls down a vineyard block at the winery.

He describes this subtle sauvignon blanc as sancerre-like. Not that he is the sort of bloke to go around making comparisons between New Zealand wines and those from the wine regions of France. But his description is apt. From 2002's devastating spring frosts and pre-harvest rains have come some of Nelson's best wines. The ruinous effects such weather conditions had reduced cropping levels, which means more concentration of flavour in the remaining grapes. Pre-harvest rains meant Finn had to leave his sauvignon blanc grapes on the vines for longer than usual. The result is a sauvignon blanc that has had the time and cool climate to develop in taste beyond impressive, upfront fruitiness into a more mature wine style.

Finn is one of the founding members of the New Zealand Screwcap Initiative, launched in 2001.

For him the jury is still out on how well red wines will taste in the long term if they are sealed with a screw cap, but he is trialling his pinot noir this way and is certain that his whites are all the better for it. This is significant in a country whose wine industry is as small as New Zealand's. Finn is one of the tiniest wine producers in a nation whose reputation for high quality far outweighs its minuscule drop into the world's wine bucket each year. But Tim and Judy Finn have more than earned their stripes as owners of one of the country's most highly respected wineries, pioneering an almost untried region in the 1970s, a time when few others could be bothered thinking beyond the appeal of Nelson as an alternative lifestyler's paradise. They have had an unerring focus on creating unforgettably good wines since the start and have created one of the most picturesque wineries in their own region and in New Zealand. The village-like appearance of the sloping property feels like it might have been there forever. It is this evocatively beautiful setting as much as the wines they make that has been most satisfying for the Finns.

Tim Finn says, 'It's the old location, location, location of the wine world. We're not talking about just producing a lot of grapes but rather of creating complexity and texture in our wines, wines which speak of our cool climate and our site.'

Since the start, they have been experimental. First, by establishing a winery in the Moutere hills area of Nelson (itself already considered to have a cool climate in a country beset with often chilly growing conditions). Then they experimented with a wide range of different grape varieties. When screw caps became available as an alternative wine seal to cork, they leapt in. And as we discuss the future of Nelson, Finn brings out his latest innovation: the first ever rosé he has made. The merlot grapes are from a contract grower's vineyard. It's not a serious wine, for many, but Finn makes every bit as much effort to create a top quality rosé as he does with his other wines.

The first people to plant grapes in Nelson were some immigrant Germans in 1843 and 1844, who were disheartened by the hard work involving in taming the land and gave up and, in 1845, headed for South Australia.

There was a gap of about 40 years before F. H. M. Ellis and sons made wine from cherries, wild blackberries and grapes. And then in the late 1960s and early 1970s, a Frenchman named Viggo du Fresne made small quantities of red wine at Ruby Bay.

Nelson has two distinctly different climates for growing grapes, each one producing fruit with vastly different flavour, structure and body.

Most Nelson grapes are grown on the Waimea Plains, of which winemaker Tim Finn says the free-draining soils are similar to those found on the Wairau Plains in Marlborough. By contrast, grapes grown on clay gravel soils in the Moutere hills enjoy a climate that is less wind-prone, has higher peak summer temperatures and cooler night temperatures than on the Waimea Plains.

This new century has also heralded the growth of Brightwater, a previously small sub-region of Nelson, and new plantings on clay based soils at Mapua, which are proving popular with winemakers intent on making bright and fresh sauvignon blancs and pinot noirs from Brightwater and weightier styles of pinot noir from Mapua.

Spring comes early to Nelson most years, with little frost risk but dependably damaging spells of gusty winds and rainy spells. Once the up-and-down spring weather is over, Nelson has reliable, settled weather until late summer. This is tempered by cool nights, which result in cool to intermediate climate flavours in the grapes.

Nelson has been saddled with its size (tiny), its grapes bought in from other regions (by some, not all, of its winemakers) and its slightly off the beaten track location. But its two distinctively different sub-regions are, more than anything else, the reason that the region as a whole has had a somewhat blurred image.

Nelson's sauvignon blancs have plenty in common with those from Marlborough, as might be expected, given that these two regions are closer in latitude than any others in New Zealand. On the Waimea Plains, grapes tend to develop intense fruity flavours, although less overt tastes of passionfruit and kiwifruit often characterise Marlborough's most distinctive sauvignon blancs. The Plains are also proving to be a reliable source of quality chardonnay and intense tasting riesling grapes.

Finn attributes the clay and gravel slopes of vineyards in the Moutere hills with the ability to provide pinot noir grapes that are dense and savoury in taste and, he claims, fuller-bodied generally than the pinot noir grown on the Plains. Conversely, chardonnay from

LEFT: Seifried Estate's vineyards are mainly on the Waimea Plains in Nelson.
ABOVE: Looking north from Nelson's Kahurangi Estate, in the Upper Moutere.

BELOW LEFT AND RIGHT: Waimea Estates, now the second biggest Nelson winery, has vineyards planted in chardonnay, riesling, sauvignon blanc, cabernet sauvignon, cabernet franc, merlot and pinot noir; the last finds its way into a fresh, summery rosé.

RIGHT: Most pinot noir vines in Nelson are young and winemakers are patiently looking forward to making wines from more mature vines, as the vineyards age.

the Moutere hills tends to taste almost lighter, more minerally in flavour and less overtly fruit driven.

Ask Tim Finn why he planted a vineyard on the clay-based soils of the Moutere hills rather than the more obvious Waimea Plains, and his answer is candidly honest and less wine oriented than many might expect. 'I wanted a hillside vineyard,' he answers with a smile.

This is far more than a romantic notion for Finn, whose Upper Moutere vineyard and winery have turned out to have an enormous advantage because of the relatively big diurnal swing in temperature (another way of saying that this region is cooler at night, often hotter during the day and generally capable of producing grapes that take longer to ripen and therefore define cool climate viticulture). And after 30 years of harnessing the best flavours that the microclimate and soils in these hills can offer in a wine, Finn admits the natural beauty of the site also appealed greatly to him and Judy Finn.

'The only thing I would change, if I could,' says Judy, 'is probably not to have had our house looking out over the vines.

'Some mornings it is too beautiful for words but it is like looking at work each day and I think of all the things we need to do.'

When Andrew Greenhough and Jenny Wheeler moved to Nelson in November 1990, it was not to escape the city but because they saw a winery for sale and wanted to make wine.

'We love cities,' says Wheeler, with the same sort of enthusiasm you might expect of somebody living on Ponsonby's café strip.

There were only four other wineries in Nelson when Greenhough and Wheeler took over the reins of the tiny Ranzau Wines, which consisted of four hectares, two of which were planted in vines and mainly in müller-thurgau with the other half gewürztraminer, cabernet sauvignon, pinot noir and riesling. Ranzau was later renamed Pelorus Wines and then it became Greenhough Winery in 1997.

One of the positives about having vines already planted when they took over was that they could make wine from day one.

It was evident from the start, say both Greenhough and Wheeler, that cabernet sauvignon was marginal, hard to ripen even in the warmer than usual years. But because they had cabernet sauvignon grapes, they used them until the mid-1990s, calling it a dry red and blending pinot noir in to override the overtly green taste of the wine.

'We persevered with cabernet by reducing bud numbers on the vines and focused on a severe pruning regime to get a low yield in order to get things right,' says Greenhough, whose mantra is that of every perfectionist winemaker: good wine is made in the vineyard.

He admits vineyard management helped but says the cabernet sauvignon was still 'second-rate stuff that was green in taste'.

Tim Finn's early attempts at cabernet sauvignon received good reviews by writers. While one suspects he might have been over the moon to have made a top-notch cabernet, Finn has long ago given up on this variety for the region, opting instead to try his hand at pinot noir.

Like Greenhough, Finn realised relatively early on that cabernet sauvignon was not going to be The Next Big Red Thing in Nelson.

'We knew our pinot noir grapes actually made quite nice wine, but we didn't come here with a mission to make world class pinot noir, initially,' says Greenhough.

Passion for pinot noir did not excite the Nelson wine scene until the late 1990s and early 2000s. While several permutations of

sauvignon blanc and chardonnay styles are the cash cows for most wineries, for Neudorf Vineyards chardonnay has been queen and king. For other Nelson wineries, riesling and pinot noir are the grapes making the most exciting, intense, regionally definitive wines.

Where pinot noir is concerned, the biggest challenge for makers in Nelson, as in other South Island wine regions, is to get the grapes physiologically ripe without having to wait till the sugars are too high.

Tim Finn describes pinot noir from Nelson as less overtly fruity than it often is in other New Zealand wine regions. But he confesses that, in some years, by waiting till the grapes are fully ripe and devoid of greenness there is a risk of higher alcohol levels than is desirable.

To help overcome this, Finn has a trial underway using a mulch of mussel shells underneath the vines to reflect light onto the grapes.

'We find that the mussel shells are reflective. Our second year of trialling this was in 2003 and the results so far have been promising enough for us to expand the trial to a commercial size,' says Finn.

He is growing a wide range of different clones of pinot noir and as each begins to produce grapes and gain vine age, his top red wine is becoming more complex – in a weighty, muscular style.

In contrast, Waimea Estates winemaker Mike Brown makes a more minerally pinot noir, from grapes grown on the Waimea Plains.

'The region's best red is easily pinot noir and Nelson pinot is underrated. If there is a commonality to these wines I would say that they have very vivid, vibrant fruit characters, but expressed with understatement rather than over-the-top aromas,' says Brown, adding that, within this, there is a vast difference between the wines grown on the plains and in the Moutere hills.

The Greenhough pinot noir is also a lighter style of wine, as its maker intends.

'The characters we have been aiming at in pinot are elegance, which I know is a clichéd word in relation to this grape but for us it is about creating a feminine wine style, as opposed to a more muscular style, and that's what I'm liking about a lot of pinots from further south,' says Greenhough.

It is well accepted by Nelson winemakers that their heavier soils tend to provide grapes with more weighty characters, whereas soils on the plains provide conditions in which the grapes develop more perfumed, aromatic, feminine styles of flavours, resulting in these sort of wines. But, as Greenhough says, providing the wines are well made, have relatively good concentration of flavour and are not just thin, then a range of stylistic differences is a good thing.

Finn adds that the noticeable rise in quality of Nelson pinot noir over the last half decade is because of improved clonal availability.

What he describes as the rather rustic tasting 10/5 pinot noir clone has given way to the more urbane, less herbaceous Pommard clone and Dijon clones.

'We want to make wines that have some restraint and have a wineyness about them, wines that are subtle and understated and complex, but not because of oak use or winemaking tricks.'

Nelson's most consistent wine is chardonnay. The most famous, Neudorf Moutere Chardonnay, is made by Tim Finn, who admits he is at a crossroads with it.

The wine has won praise and fame, but it is now on the verge of major change because of new – and, Finn says, extremely good tasting – chardonnay clones.

'Mendosa was our initial chardonnay clone and is still our favourite, giving us grapes with that concentrated, mineral style. Having said that, clones 95 and 8021 are showing excellent promise in their second year, in a broader, and intriguingly perfumed, style.'

So far, so great. Unfortunately, the blend of the Mendosa clone with these relative newcomers is not as distinctive as its individual parts, which means that Finn will probably introduce a new premium chardonnay label to accommodate the broader styled clones.

In a more subtle but distinctively big bodied style is winemaker Phil Jones' Tasman Bay Chardonnay, made in minuscule quantities but with a stylish flourish of tropical fruit tastes coupled with creamy texture which is not at all over the top in style. Jones' winery is tucked away in a particularly beautiful corner of the country in the Moutere hills.

Riesling is a work in progress here, as elsewhere in New Zealand, with some winemakers taking it extremely seriously and others using it as an extra string to their vinous bows.

The winemaker paying most homage to this undoubtedly great variety is Andrew Greenhough, who crops grapes at the relatively low 1.2 tonnes to the hectare. 'To go below that level seems to be a bit silly, economically,' he says.

Greenhough's riesling vines range in age from one-year-old to 24-year-old vines and the styles of rieslings he wants to make range from dry to sweet. Most have been at the dry end of the spectrum

LEFT: Experimental mulch from New Zealand's plentiful supplies of green-lipped mussels helps to reflect heat back onto grapevines at Neudorf Vineyards.
ABOVE: Nelson, in the north-west of the South Island, is heaven for those who enjoy the great outdoors, with perfect sea conditions for kayaking, rivers to canoe and fish in, and many dramatic walks and tramps in the mountain ranges.

but also a little higher in alcohol levels than Greenhough wants. To overcome this, he plans to pick riesling grapes at a wider range of sugar levels in order to get a dry style of wine at a lower than usual alcohol level.

For the winemaker and winery owner of Woollaston Estates, Philip Woollaston, the riesling grape is also the brightest white hope on Nelson's wine horizon because, in his words, it is so distinctive in its taste.

'For me, Nelson riesling has more spine and better acid balance than many from other regions in New Zealand,' says Woollaston, who also puts significant effort into producing good chardonnay and sauvignon blanc.

The biggest challenge presented by Nelson for making wine is that of coming to terms with the region's terroir, says Finn.

What Finn means when he talks about terroir is getting to grips in a specific sense, as well as a broad one, with which grapes grow best in which soils, microclimates and terrains in this wine region. And this is not about to happen overnight, given that it took him two decades to understand not only what his Moutere hills vineyards give to one clone of chardonnay but now to a whole range of different chardonnay grapes.

His first vintage in Nelson was in 1981 and Finn says it took all of that decade 'to get some understanding of how to handle the vines in the Moutere terroir'.

As far as marketing Nelson wine goes, a new brand called Wineart was launched in late 2003 to define the synergy that exists in the region between the wineries, lifestylers and artists.

The biggest problem is that, while Nelson as a region can and does produce world class wines over a range of different varieties, it does not have a perceived focus on any one variety or style for the public or wine writers to seize on.

As the region grows, each sub-area will gain enough mass to present its own image. Nelson has three percent of the country's vineyard and is expanding rapidly. Not least because Seifried Estate, the largest Nelson winery in 2003, has now taken the strategic step of not buying in grapes from other regions.

Seifried Estate began when Hermann Seifried moved to Nelson to make apple wine for the New Zealand Apple and Pear Board, in the 1970s.

'It didn't take me long to work out that I did not want to waste

ABOVE: Waimea Estates vineyards are now second only to Nelson's Seifried Estate in terms of size and annual production. RIGHT: Winemaker Mike Brown was attracted to the region because of the chance to work with his two favourite grape varieties: riesling and pinot noir. Brown admits he was a complete neophyte with both grapes, in terms of making wine from them. FAR RIGHT: Jenny Wheeler and Andrew Greenhough bought the small Ranzau winery in 1991, home at the time to just 1.5 hectares of vines, which they have replanted and extended today for their top quality oriented Greenhough Vineyard and Winery.

my time on apple wine when this place had such a great climate for growing grapes,' says the Austrian-born, German-trained winemaker.

Since his first vintage in 1976, Seifried and his New Zealand-born wife, Agnes, have tried their hands at everything from sylvaner to sauvignon blanc, several permutations of chardonnay, riesling and a consistently good, surprisingly affordable gewürztraminer that wings its way out of the winery to all over New Zealand each year. And then there are Seifried's reds, including cabernet sauvignon, merlot, pinot noir and, now, zweigelt, a late ripening Austrian grape variety. 'It may not seem like the most logical thing to plant in Nelson but I like zweigelt and it is experimental plantings like these that make it worth getting up in the morning,' laughs Seifried.

Seifried often comes across as a quirky experimentalist but he is also an ambitious pragmatist.

He and Agnes began their winery in Upper Moutere as Weingut Seifried at the facility that is now owned by Kahurangi Estate.

'He added on and added on and eventually it became obvious we needed a far, far bigger winery,' smiles Agnes. So in 1993 they opened their vast new winery about midway between Upper Moutere and the city of Nelson, at Appleby. Since then they have increased their vine plantings on the Waimea Plains and pioneered vineyards at Brightwater. Until recently they continued to buy in grapes from Marlborough, to supplement production.

'We did not get the best grapes that we could from Marlborough and when we assessed our situation and saw our kids head into the business with us, we decided to start building a winery that was truly Nelson-based.'

Now they are determined to be a true-only-to-Nelson winery and are also putting an increasing emphasis on sustainable viticulture.

'We restrict the use of copper and organic fungicides in order to look after the environment rather than to gain organic certification, although that is not out of the question, but it would be a long way in the future,' explains Agnes Seifried.

With 170 hectares planted, the Seifrieds are focusing mainly on sauvignon blanc, which makes up half of their production. They also make pinot noir, chardonnay and smaller amounts of other wines from riesling, gewürztraminer, malbec, syrah, cabernet sauvignon and pinot gris. Around 50 percent of all of their wine is exported.

Waimea Estates is knocking on the door of Seifried, in terms of size, but it started life as a contract grape-growing company.

Owners Trevor and Robyn Bolitho have grown grapes since 1993, initially mainly for Corbans Wines (once the second largest winery in New Zealand; now owned by the biggest, Montana Wines).

Sauvignon blanc is big for Waimea Estates, where it accounts for more than 50 percent of total annual wine production, followed by pinot noir with about 15 per cent and then chardonnay and riesling.

In good years winemakers Mike Brown and Wietske van der Pol also make pinot gris, gewürztraminer and syrah – 'Just a tiny little bit, a smidgeon for a bit of fun really,' explains van der Pol of the syrah.

Another just-for-fun wine made at Waimea Estates is the rosé, made from pinot noir and sold mainly at the winery.

Woollaston Estates is the brainchild of Philip Woollaston, who established the tiny Wai-Iti River Vineyard in 1996. From the start this quietly spoken former MP and mayor of Nelson has made a big splash with small quantities of limey tasting riesling.

Now, he has taken on an investment partner, American resort hotelier Glenn Schaeffer. Together they have formed Woollaston Estates with control over 90 hectares of vineyard land, planted in sauvignon blanc, pinot noir, riesling, chardonnay and cabernet sauvignon from the Brightwater area to Mahana (on the ridge between Mapua and Upper Moutere), Kelling Road vineyard in Upper Moutere and Burke's Bank vineyard by the Wairoa River.

In 2003 they were also constructing a gravity-fed winery.

It's a far cry from the little retirement project that Woollaston's wife, Chan, persuaded him a smallish vineyard would be, but he is not one to do things by halves. And if his early attempts at riesling and current output of high quality sauvignon blanc are even a vague indication, this is a winery that will wow drinkers in years to come.

Expansion is occurring in Nelson in a multitude of very different ways, from the massive investment going into Woollaston Estates and the head of steam that Seifried already has through to smaller wineries operating on closely managed contracts with independent grape-growers.

The unerring emphasis on top quality by the region's smallest producers is finally starting to give impetus to big wineries in Nelson. And although this sun-drenched region is tucked into a particularly leisure-focused region of New Zealand, the winemakers here could not be more serious about making quality-focused wines that can foot it with the best in the country and the world.

ABOVE: Austrian-born Hermann Seifried is one of Nelson's wine pioneers, who made his first wine from the region in 1976 from the sylvaner grape. Seifreid Estate's winery at Rabbit Island is home to 55 hectares of vines, with other extensive plantings in Nelson's sub-regions.
RIGHT: Spraying is part of life for most grape-growers, many of whom are intentionally lowering the amount and frequency of their spraying regimes, as part of the Sustainable Winegrowing New Zealand programme, initiated by New Zealand Winegrowers.

Nelson wineries

Brightwater Vineyards

Main Road, Brightwater, Nelson, phone (03) 544 1066

Denton Winery

135 Awa Awa Road, Upper Moutere, RD 1, Nelson, phone (03) 540 3555

Fossil Ridge

161 Hill Street, Richmond, Nelson, phone (03) 544 7459

Glover's Vineyard

Gardner Valley Road, RD 1, Upper Moutere, Nelson, phone (03) 543 2698

Greenhough Vineyard & Winery

Patons Road, Hope, Nelson, phone (03) 542 3868

Holmes Brothers winery

McShanes Road, Richmond, Nelson, phone (03) 544 4230

Kahurangi Estate

Sunrise Road, Upper Moutere, Nelson, phone (03) 543 2980

Kaimira Estate

121 River Terrace Road, RD 1, Brightwater, Nelson, phone (03) 542 3431

Le Gros Family Vines

124 River Terrace Road, RD 1, Brightwater, Nelson, phone (03) 542 3408

McCashin's Wines

664 Main Road, Stoke, Nelson, phone (03) 547 0205

Moutere Hills Vineyard

Sunrise Valley, RD 1, Upper Moutere, Nelson, phone (03) 543 2288

Neudorf Vineyards

Neudorf Road, Upper Moutere, Nelson, phone (03) 543 2643

Rimu Grove Winery

Bronte Road East, RD 1, Upper Moutere, Nelson, phone (03) 540 2345

Seifried Estate

Redwood Road, Appleby, Nelson, phone (03) 544 5599

Spencer Hill Estate

Best Road, Upper Moutere, phone (03) 543 2031

Stafford Lane Estate

80 Moutere Highway, RD 1, Richmond, Nelson, phone (03) 544 2851

Sunset Valley Vineyard

Eggers Road, RD 1, Upper Moutere, Nelson, phone (03) 543 2161

Te Mania Estate

Pughs Road, RD 1, Richmond, Nelson, phone (03) 544 4541

Waimea Estates

148 Main Road, Hope, Nelson, phone (03) 544 6385

Woollaston Estates

243 Old Coach Road, RD 1, Upper Moutere, Nelson, phone (03) 542 3205

Marlborough

Hard as it is to believe, just three decades ago some in the New Zealand wine industry argued that the South Island was too cold a place in which to grow grapes. And when the first commercial vineyard was planted in Marlborough in 1973, others claimed it would never work. Today Marlborough is not only New Zealand's largest wine region, it is the most powerful. Its winemakers wield strong influence over the style of New Zealand wine and produce more of it for both domestic and global sales than any other regions in this country. Pinot noir has overtaken chardonnay as Marlborough's second most planted grape but sauvignon blanc, New Zealand's most planted variety, is still in first place.

It is a very cold, very wet afternoon, and outside it is pitch black, even though it is only 4 pm. In my favourite wine glass is a lightly chilled Marlborough sauvignon blanc, which reminds me of how ridiculously sunny the biggest wine region in New Zealand actually is. It is easy to forget a detail like this when you are living in the abysmally cold climate of a northern hemisphere winter like this one in Edinburgh, when in the early 1990s I finally fell for the unique taste of New Zealand sauvignon blanc.

Marlborough sauvignon blanc, more than any other white wine made in this country, is so instantly recognisable, so piercingly fresh and surprisingly pungent that it is easy to take such wine for granted if you are a New Zealander.

It was also a cold and windy day when grapes were first planted in this region on a large scale. Winemaker Allan Scott recalls with vivid embarrassment over-watering the motley collection of grapevines that would one day make this region and the country famous far beyond the actual scale of wine produced here.

In August 1973 Allan Scott and 80-odd others stuck the first of many twig-like vines in the ground and hoped for the best. Like many who have become involved in wine, Scott had moved to Marlborough not to make wine but to grow trees and when the opportunity to work for Montana Wines came along it looked far more interesting than forestry.

PREVIOUS PAGES: The iconic and aptly named Wither Hills, which always appear as a dry and barren backdrop to many Marlborough vineyards.
ABOVE: Cloudy Bay's sauvignon blanc grapes are among the most highly sought after around the world.
RIGHT: Marlborough vineyards are planted on relatively youthful soils, most of which are just 14,000 years old, mere babes in terms of soil age.

'The biggest challenge is that the wine industry is very disproportionate. There are very few people who are passionate about it and a lot who have come on board because they think it's the thing to do.'   Allan Scott, Allan Scott Wines

'We were novices,' says Scott. 'Nobody knew anything about viticulture apart from Jim Hamilton, who was sent from a vineyard he managed up north for Montana Wines, but we all gave it a go.'

After just three weeks, Scott had become one of the leading hands in Montana's Marlborough crew. Even now, he describes it as 'a bit of a crazy thing', which happened purely because he had shown more interest than some others and it was such early days.

'There was a fair bit of antipathy to the South Island planting thing and people were saying it was a bit of a joke and it was too cold. I knew it would work because my parents-in-law here had grapes and citrus that were thriving,' Scott says.

Like others in the region, Allan Scott's biggest learning curve was being given responsibility for something he knew very little about. So he started reading anything and everything he could lay his hands on

about grapes and wines. One of the most important books was by a former government viticulturist, Frank Berry-Smith, whose book was penned in 1947 but was still, says Scott, 'incredibly applicable'.

'The thing that struck me was that viticulture is pretty basic and very straightforward. You want the best material you can find and then you plant it.'

As straightforward as that was, it took until the end of the 1970s, says Scott, for most in the industry back then to figure out how to get sufficient moisture to new vines to get them growing. By then the capital expenditure in the experiment was way out of control, says Scott, and the realisation had dawned for some that the most planted grapes, müller-thurgau and cabernet sauvignon, were possibly not the most suitable. The most important thing was that grapes for wine could be grown successfully in Marlborough.

As he went on to prove in several roles – supervisor of Montana's Fairhall Vineyard, overseeing the establishment of Corbans Wines' Marlborough vineyards and as a viticultural consultant – Scott has helped to pioneer not only the region but many of its most important grape varieties. Today the Allan Scott sauvignon blanc and riesling are among Marlborough's best examples of these varieties, with pinot noir evolving into a headier, more weighty style with each year.

Marlborough conjures up curvaceous sounds, rolling hills, rocky rivers and grassy plains for most New Zealanders. The region's position at the north-eastern tip of the South Island means Marlborough's vineyards are a mix of silt over free-draining loams and, on the region's hottest vineyards, stony gravel washed by rivers across the Wairau Plains. Vineyards have spread from the river flats and drained swampland of the plains to adjacent river valleys where most of the region's grapes are planted: in the Wairau Valley, Waihopai and Awatere.

The first wine grapes known to be grown in Marlborough were planted in 1875 in hills south of Fairhall and Brancott by David Herd, who made a sweet red wine from muscatel grapes. More grapes were planted in Marlborough near Picton in 1880, when George Freeth began churning out wine made from both grapes and other fruits that he grew. Two other men became involved in the region's early wine scene. Harry Patchett and Mansoor Peters grew grapes and sold wine in Marlborough in the first half of the twentieth century. As luck would have it, Patchett lived until 1974, just long enough to see Montana Wines pioneer a modern wave of Marlborough winemaking.

There were other pioneers whose role was as significant as those early plantings by Montana Wines in 1973.

Ernie Hunter sowed the seeds of Hunter's Wines, one of Marlborough's largest and best known wineries today, in 1983 when he built a winery at Rapaura.

Like all the successful early pioneers, it was Hunter's sauvignon blanc that wine drinkers first took notice of in the early 1980s and, as time has gone on, it is still one of the best in the region. Ernie's life was ended in 1987 in a tragic car accident, after which his wife Jane Hunter took over running the winery. She is still at the helm today and, like her late husband, is a vociferous supporter of the region and the country as well as her own wines.

It was the dream of Australian winemaker David Hohnen to be involved in Marlborough. When Hohnen, a part-owner of Cape

LEFT: Some of New Zealand's most famous sauvignon blanc vines at Cloudy Bay Vineyards on Jacksons Road in Blenheim.
ABOVE: Establishing the region as a wine producer and then their own vineyards and winery has been hugely rewarding for Allan Scott (pictured) and his wife Catherine, and now their children are involved.

Mentelle winery in Western Australia, got involved in Marlborough in the mid-1980s, there was only a winemaker called Kevin Judd – still there today.

Judd pioneered the vineyards, the winery and the top-notch sauvignon blanc from this region. For many, it was the very stylish branding of Cloudy Bay wines – a direct emulation of the successful Australian Cape Mentelle label – that put Cloudy Bay onto the wine map. But everyone in the wine industry knows it was and is the intensity of taste and impeccable balance of Cloudy Bay Sauvignon Blanc that gave it the edge right from the start. The winery is one of the region's biggest today and definitely one of the most successful producers of sparkling wine in two distinctly different styles – a subtle and crisp chardonnay-driven bubbly and a yeasty, fresh pinot noir bubbly. Cloudy Bay's pinot noir is one of the best in the region, though Judd will say its style is still evolving. And the sauvignon blanc … it is still either the best or one of them every single year.

Marlborough's vineyard has more than doubled

in size since 1999, when there were 3400 hectares of vines planted. That figure was forecast to be 7679 hectares by the end of 2004, with more growth predicted.

Not surprisingly, Montana Wines – the biggest winery in the region – has about a third of the area's vines as well as sourcing grapes from contract growers, paid by the winery to supply grapes.

With the increased scarcity of suitable vineyard land in Marlborough, Montana Wines' future growth will probably be mainly from existing grape-growers.

'We are looking for more suitable land but putting emphasis on contract growers and also concentrating a lot of our new plantings in the Waipara region in North Canterbury,' says Montana Marlborough winery manager, Gerry Gregg.

'There is not a lot of land left since we already have land within the two main valleys. A lot of the other areas in Marlborough that have not yet been planted are very marginal, in terms of climate and water shortage. A lot of the land in the southern valleys of the Wairau Valley has also to date been restricted by a lack of water, but with a new community water scheme being put in place, some marginal land may become suitable for growing grapes on,' says Gregg.

Marlborough's biggest strength is its climate.

Cool maritime growing conditions are tempered by long, dry, hot summer days. Even on one of these plentiful days when you feel like removing most of your clothing, the evenings in Marlborough are so

ABOVE FAR LEFT: Viticulturist Ivan Sutherland inspects grapes at Cloudy Bay's home vineyard block, next to the Blenheim winery.
ABOVE LEFT: Neatly trimmed rows of grapes in Marlborough, New Zealand's largest wine region and destined to stay that way with forecast growth from 44 percent of the national vineyard area in 2003 to 48 percent by 2006.
LEFT BELOW: Sauvignon blanc is the country's and this region's most planted grape variety, constituting 56 percent – and growing – of all Marlborough's vineyard area.
ABOVE: Grapes nearly ready for harvest at Cloudy Bay in Marlborough.

cool that residents and visitors alike are reaching for their woollies. In part, this is due to the nearby mountain ranges that flank the region to the east. During the day the vineyards closest to the coast are cooled by sea breezes, but these areas are also prone to potentially damaging humidity in seasons of high rain. Marlborough's climate is generally drier than many other wine areas in New Zealand but it does not avoid the risk of botrytis and other rots when the rain starts.

The biggest challenge in Marlborough is the change in climate, according to some winemakers.

Summers have become hotter and, because water is in short supply, some grapes are parched and vines close down during the ripening phase, according to veteran winemaker Allan Scott. Weather patterns tend to be cyclical but Scott says the current trend of very hot summers is becoming a trial to winemakers who are trying to achieve consistency in the style of their wines.

Heat, says Allan Scott, is only part of the ripening process. Also key to vine growth and development of flavour within grapes is light.

'In the past we tended to get the grapes riper and riper and riper until they lost that dash of zippiness that always defined Marlborough sauvignon blanc. Now we are moving back to trying to enhance those unique flavours.'

Not all of Marlborough's soils are considered to be well suited for grape-growing and there is a wide variation of both stony, gravelly based soils and more fertile sandy loams in the region. In the Awatere Valley, slightly south and inland of Blenheim township, soils are a mixture of gravel and silty loams with a smattering of deep, free-draining, loamy soils.

Marlborough's most recently pioneered sub-region is the Seventeen Valley, also just south of Blenheim township but closer to

'To make the most exciting wines from Marlborough, you have got to be here for the long haul. We are, especially in relation to pinot noir.' Kevin Judd, Cloudy Bay Vineyards

the coast than the Awatere. The vineyards here are owned by a trio of wine lovers, including, principally, John Buchanan, who planted the land in grapes in 1997. Buchanan says that Seventeen Valley is a little warmer than most parts of Marlborough. His winery is Mount Riley Wines, jointly owned by winemaker Digger (aka Bill Hennessy) and a silent partner.

Ironically, Buchanan bought the land at Seventeen Valley mainly for pinot noir and while it does constitute most of the plantings, there is also a little chardonnay, cabernet sauvignon and merlot. Seventeen Valley is run at low yields, always picked at less than two tonnes to the acre, following a strict pruning and thinning regime, dropping fruit prior to harvest, in order to ensure that the remaining grapes are intense in taste and few in number. Unusually, for Marlborough, all of the grapes from the Seventeen Valley vineyard are hand-picked and none are inoculated with yeast but rather allowed to ferment with the yeasts present in the atmosphere. The wines are whole-bunch pressed, which gives less juice but also less phenolic influence, resulting in generally smooth and silky-textured wines. Mount Riley chardonnay is totally barrel-fermented and the pinot noir is all hand-plunged, with no pumping over at all, prior to a rigorous barrel selection. The sauvignon blanc is barrel-fermented, in old oak (usually at least five years old, according to Buchanan), in order to allow a little contact with oxygen rather than imbue the wine with any actual oak taste. These gentle winemaking techniques are part of Buchanan and Hennessy's quest to make the absolute best wines they can from the grapes grown.

Then there is the oldest slice of land in Marlborough, currently being planted in the Waihopai Valley. When it is fully planted, around 2015, Bankhouse Station will be the largest vineyard in the country, and may attain this distinction even earlier than that. It is on the oldest soils in Marlborough, on an enormous old river terrace at the confluence of the Wairau and Waihopai rivers on the site of a former farm.

This project is the idea of viticulturist Damian Martin and wine marketer Martin Cahnbley, who worked at the now-defunct Corbans Wines when that company still existed in its own right.

The drawcard of this property is that it is delineated on all sides, making it a clearly differentiated geological entity with its own soil types and mesoclimate.

'The vineyards on flat land in the rest of Marlborough are planted on soils that are less than a thousand years old. In contrast, this area has soils that are ten to twenty thousand years old,' says Martin.

LEFT: The Awatere Valley, south of Blenheim, is one of the coolest sub-regions in Marlborough and home to a growing number of new ventures.
BELOW: Standing in the Mount Riley vineyard in the Seventeen Valley, south of Blenheim township, are John Buchanan and wine-maker Digger Hennessy, co-owners in the winery.

The duo's vision for their new vineyard is to see it become a recognised sub-region within Marlborough.

'A lot of people in the wine industry talk about appellations but we want to take a fresh look at the whole appellation concept and put a much more New World stamp on it, in order to create a concept that wine drinkers will understand that sums up this area.'

That flavour will relate mostly to the region's two most planted grape varieties, sauvignon blanc and pinot noir, with a sprinkling of other varieties planted – perhaps.

Martin is mapping this new area's soil variability in conjunction with Massey University. Electromagnetic sensing measures the soil conductivity and while Martin admits it is not a perfect science – 'You need to plant the vineyard to know what that conductivity means in terms of vine performance and grape flavours' – it does allow them to match like with like. This means planting grape varieties in soil types on slopes or flat areas and in climatic zones that best suit them. The next extension of this is matching the right rootstocks to grape varieties and, in turn, matching them to specific pieces of land.

It sounds impressive but one gigantic winery is not in the pipeline, the pair insist.

Cahnbley says: 'We want to create a union of producers with their own expressions of identity from this sub-region. We are not talking about one mega-brand coming out of here but rather about the creation of an environment that is recognised, globally, as having a specific taste.'

The greatest white in Marlborough is sauvignon blanc. Its rise to fame came out of the blue. Many winemakers in other countries have tried to imitate the flavour but with limited and, it has to be said, dilute success. As well as launching a new taste, three key wineries – Cloudy Bay, Hunter's Wines and Montana Wines – also marketed the country and its beauty in their evocative labels and images of forever-blue, sunny skies. While Cloudy Bay and Hunter's Wines had more than their fair share of marketing coups, Montana Wines backed that up by providing Marlborough sauvignon blanc in quantity and uniformly high in quality. It also commanded a relatively high price tag, but still within reach for many consumers in New Zealand's biggest export market to date, the United Kingdom.

Ownership and management of grapevines is often a contentious issue for grape-growers and winemakers. Most winemakers say that having control over their own grapes is intrinsic to wine quality.

ABOVE: Aerial shot of Montana Wines' Brancott Vineyard, which hosts the annual Marlborough Wine and Food Festival, New Zealand's oldest celebration of the grape.
RIGHT: Montana Wines' Brancott Vineyard is New Zealand's largest and one of its oldest, covering enormous tracts of flat ground with small pockets planted on slopes.

For the relatively large Babich Wines, the ratio of grapes from owned vineyards to contract grapes bought in has recently adjusted from 50/50 to being 70 percent owned vineyards and 30 percent bought in.

'We would rather not expand vineyards because wineries absorb so much money, but the supply of grapes is a strategic item from a quality, supply and price point of view,' says David Babich, assistant general manager and third-generation family member of Babich Wines.

At Saint Clair Estate Wines it is a different story. Until three years ago, this relatively large New Zealand winery used only one contract grape-grower; now they have 25 growers who contribute about 50 percent of the total wine production at Saint Clair. Far from lowering wine quality, the nature of this type of expansion has helped to boost it, says Saint Clair owner Neal Ibbotson.

For Ibbotson, having so many contract grape-growers from a wide range of sub-regions within Marlborough means that he has greater accessibility to different flavours than ever before.

He insists that it is fertile, deep and free-draining soils as opposed to the stony soils that provide the best sauvignon blanc grapes. His preferred vineyards are also on the cooler sites in the region, on which he opts for longer 'hang times' leaving the grapes on the vines until he considers their flavours to be at their very best.

'If you have wide variation of different soils and microclimates within a vineyard, you will have a wide variation in flavours, so it is extremely hard to decide when the flavours are at their best, but that is our biggest challenge.'

Such decisions are made in the mouth and on foot. Like most winemakers prior to harvest time each year, Ibbotson and his team walk the rows making decisions on the day as to whether the grapes taste good enough to be ready to pick.

Sauvignon blanc forms the backbone of Babich Wines, which is based in Auckland but sources more than half of its grapes in Marlborough, where it part-owns a winemaking facility. (A substantial proportion of Babich wines is made with grapes grown in Hawke's Bay, where its chardonnays, cabernet sauvignon and merlot-based reds come from.)

The quality of Babich Wines is uniformly high, which David Babich attributes to having the right grape varieties planted on the

right vineyards in the right regions, which means that Marlborough sauvignon blanc is king and queen of Babich Wines, making up more than half of their entire production.

One of Marlborough's best sauvignon blancs is made by Brent Marris at Wither Hills winery, which was sold to the global corporate Lion Nathan in 2002. Just for the record, neither the talented and dedicated winemaker, Brent, nor his father, John, the viticulturist, have left the company. The only change under the new ownership will be a reduction in their stress levels and an increase in their bank accounts, insist the father-son partnership.

Since 2000, Wither Hills has grown from one of more than 300 tiny New Zealand wineries into a medium-sized one. Wine quality has

FAR LEFT: Chardonnay grapes freshly harvested from Daniel Le Brun's vineyard, in Allan Scott's auger.
LEFT: Virginie, one of Daniel Le Brun's bubblies.
BELOW: Frenchman Daniel Le Brun, one of New Zealand's leading pioneers of quality sparkling wine and now owner and winemaker at Le Brun Family Estate winery on Rapaura Road, Blenheim.

Brent Marris' Wither Hills Sauvignon Blanc is a successful mix of intense Marlborough fruitiness, coupled with a modern, fleshy style of wine that just begs for seafood to eat with it.

not suffered, despite the increase in size. This is partly due to the fact that there are only three wines in the Wither Hills stable: chardonnay, pinot noir and the all-important sauvignon blanc, which Brent makes by fermenting a small proportion in oak in order to add mouthfeel and texture to the wine. It works.

His sauvignon blanc is a successful intermingling of intense Marlborough fruity flavours and modern, texturally driven style.

As important as sauvignon blanc is in Marlborough, the region clearly has strong potential with other white grapes, not least of which is chardonnay, the second most planted white grape. Aromatic whites like pinot gris and riesling also have untapped potential.

'New' is definitely the most applicable description of pinot gris, which has only been made as a varietal wine in its own right since the late 1990s in New Zealand.

Nautilus winemaker Clive Jones made his third pinot gris in 2002 with grapes from two different vineyards: one in the Wairau Valley, the other in the Awatere Valley. Each vineyard contributed different tastes to the finished wine. The Awatere grapes taste citrusy and overtly fruity while those from the Wairau Valley, in this instance, added something more subtle to the wine, which was fermented to be just off-dry in style but still reached a hefty 14 percent alcohol. And therein lies the rub.

Like pinot gris from other New Zealand wine regions, levels of dryness vary vastly from one wine to the next while alcohol levels tend to be relatively high. While winemakers struggle to get to grips with what a national style of pinot gris might taste like, wine drinkers have embraced its (sometimes vague) aromatic appeal, relatively dry and often full-bodied style.

Large quantities of pinot gris are made in Marlborough by two of the country's biggest wineries, Nobilo and Villa Maria.

For wine drinkers, pinot gris is the pretty newcomer to the New Zealand white wine scene, which makes riesling a little like the ugly duckling – except for those few who know and love it.

In 2005, there was nearly twice as much riesling as pinot gris planted but it is growing at a slower rate, due to the confused image that riesling has suffered globally. And yet when it is good, riesling is, for some, the greatest white wine on the planet.

Framingham winemaker Andrew Hedley makes four different styles of riesling from bone-dry to the winery's Classic Riesling (a medium, off-dry style), a botrytis-infected noble riesling (dessert wine) and, the newest wine in the range, the Select Riesling.

ABOVE: Cloudy Bay is one of several big-name wineries with vineyards and production facilities on the now-famous Jacksons Road.
RIGHT: Swiss winemaker Hans Herzog checks brix levels at the tiny vineyard he owns with his wife, Therese.
FAR RIGHT: Mike Allan takes a sample of fermenting grape juice out of a barrel at Huia Wines, which he owns with his wife, Claire.

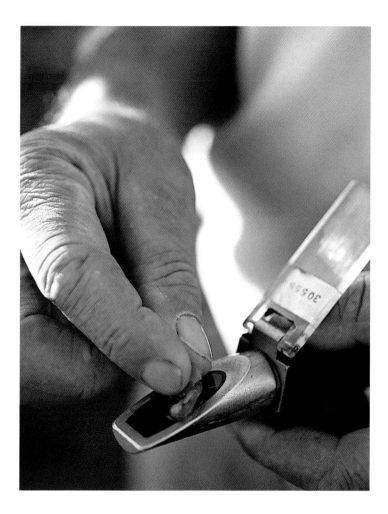

Without even trying, Marlborough winemakers have had almost unmitigated success with the riesling grape, with Babich Marlborough Riesling and Framingham Dry Riesling being two notable examples that consistently taste impressive when first made and over time as they develop into honeyed-tasting white wines.

This last wine is made from grapes that were hand-picked and whole-bunch pressed, the most gentle processing technique. The fermentation was stopped when the alcohol level reached just 8.5 percent, leaving a good whack of sugar and lots of acid to keep the wine in check. Essentially, this wine is made in the mould of a top quality German spatlese or auslese, meaning that while the sugars left in the wine post-fermentation are relatively high, they are well balanced by the corresponding acids. Overriding any classification of style, it is a definitely New Zealand wine, in terms of flavour, says Hedley, a self-declared riesling fanatic.

For the Select Riesling, bunches of grapes were selected based on colour, as is the case in similar styles of wine made in Germany.

At the time of writing, Hedley had just attended a wine seminar about riesling in London at the New Zealand Winegrowers' annual tasting for wine trade and media. And in answer to the question: which white wine has the most untapped potential in Marlborough, he unequivocally says, 'Riesling.'

'It is such a fantastically versatile variety, being happy in a wide diversity of styles and so capable of ageing well too, even though it gets a bad rap from most consumers.

'People overseas have been telling us for years that the Framingham Classic Riesling is lovely, but we will never be able to sell it, and while pinot gris is very fashionable in New Zealand now, riesling beats it hands down for me.'

What needs to happen with riesling, says Hedley and the small number of other winemakers who see the high potential with this grape, is for it to be cropped at lower levels than is currently the case. More leaf-plucking, more intensive labour and more general attention to detail with riesling is what will raise its quality – and therefore the price – helping consumers to see the potential to a greater extent than is currently the case.

Now that Marlborough has cemented its reputation for creating the world's most distinctive expression of sauvignon blanc, pinot noir has moved stealthily into second place, in terms of vines planted. It is the most widely planted red grape variety in Marlborough, which makes perfect sense for most winemakers.

As Cloudy Bay's founding winemaker and now general manager, Kevin Judd, puts it, a red must be found to equal the success of sauvignon blanc.

In outstandingly warm vintages, like the wildcard that was 1998, Marlborough can ripen merlot, cabernet sauvignon, cabernet franc and malbec grapes to a high standard. Most years, however, the best Marlborough red wines are those made from pinot noir and, in tiny quantities, also from syrah.

One of the first pinot noirs made in the region was produced at Fromm Winery in 1994 by Swiss immigrant winemaker Hatsch Kalberer. From day one, Fromm was set up to make red wine and owners Georg and Ruth Fromm hedged their bets by planting eight different red grape varieties: cabernet franc, cabernet sauvignon, malbec, merlot, montepulciano, pinot noir, sangiovese and syrah. The survivors are pinot noir, merlot and syrah.

It is pinot noir that has made the biggest mark for this winery, which Kalberer puts down to low yields of grapes, all of which are hand-picked and processed 'extremely gently at the winery'.

While the first 10 years at Fromm were about getting the basics right – which grapes to grow and where to grow them – the next 10 years will be about the health of the vineyard.

Like many in the region, Kalberer says he is only just beginning to learn how to create good soil health.

'An organic or biodynamic tag is not important but rather the knowledge of how to work in harmony with the environment instead of struggling against it.'

Most big-name Marlborough wineries have had to struggle in most years to ripen cabernet sauvignon sufficiently for a consistent red wine, which is why Judd from Cloudy Bay now describes pinot noir as the most suitable red grape variety for the region.

ABOVE: New vineyards are being planted so fast in Marlborough that annual growth is nearing 20 percent some years.
RIGHT: Montana's giant winery and visitor centre sits against this arid backdrop, which is typical of Marlborough.

For most in Marlborough, the greatest challenge will be to find ready and willing markets globally to soak up all the wine that the region's current vineyard growth will result in.

'As new clones of pinot noir come into production, we get more options from which to blend and tweak the style that we are making. And, as our vineyards gain maturity also, we can look forward to some very exciting wines made from pinot noir.'

One of the newest wineries in Marlborough is the tiny Herzog Wine Collection, owned by Swiss couple Hans and Therese Herzog, who moved their Michelin-starred restaurant lock, stock and a container-load of wine cellar from Switzerland to Marlborough. Over 1500 bottles of European wine came with them in 2000, along with all of their cutlery, plates, furniture, fittings and art. They have a strong focus on pinot noir and work meticulously in their vineyards to create what Therese describes as 'a typical Bordeuax red', made from merlot, cabernet franc, cabernet sauvignon and malbec.

Tiny quantities of the big-berried Italian grape montepulciano are also grown at the small Herzog vineyard. Montepulciano is also made at Framingham and has been trialled elsewhere in Marlborough.

One of the newest pinot noir vineyards in Marlborough belongs to Babich Wines and is situated in Cowslip Valley, a side-arm off the Waihopai Valley, which is slightly colder in spring and a bit hotter in summer than their other vineyard in the Wairau Valley.

'We were uncertain whether pinot noir would go better at the top or the bottom of this valley vineyard, so we planted it at both ends,' says David Babich.

Just as this book was going to print, Montana Wines launched its 2002 Montana Terraces Pinot Noir onto the New Zealand market. It is this winery's first attempt at a top quality pinot noir, made with grapes grown on a small ridge adjacent to one of the country's

biggest vineyards, Brancott Estate in Marlborough, situated at the southern end of the cool Wairau Valley. For the first vintage, some grapes were blended in from older pinot noir vines on the nearby Fairhall Estate, but as the grapes on the Terraces vineyard mature, they will increase as a proportion of the blended wine. It was an impressive pinot noir but Montana senior winemaker Patrick Materman says it only hints at what is possible from Marlborough.

Not every winery is stuck on pinot noir. And while words like green and herbaceous have been used with gay abandon to describe reds made from merlot and cabernet sauvignon grapes grown in Marlborough, some wineries are getting higher quality than in the past. Herzog's new addition of a cabernet sauvignon-based red is a costly exercise – both to the winemaker and the consumer – but it proves that good things can come to perfectionists who prefer to mould cabernet sauvignon from this region.

Saint Clair Estate's Rapaura Road vineyard also suits merlot well, producing grapes that make a ripe-tasting wine, and there are plenty of other examples, but cabernet sauvignon and merlot plantings have declined while pinot noir has grown and continues to do so.

Marlborough's three biggest wineries are not based in the region, although they each have vast production facilities there. Montana Wines has its biggest winery and visitor centre in Marlborough, in an unmissable chateau look-alike building on the state highway south of Blenheim township.

Villa Maria and the Nobilo Wine Group also have large wineries in the region. For each, sauvignon blanc is the most widely produced grape and all are experimenting with a wide range of pinot noir clones as well as producing chardonnay, pinot gris, riesling and bubbly.

Marlborough is the biggest wine region in New Zealand and its forecast growth will see the region have nearly 50 percent of the country's national vineyard by 2006. Currently it has 8193 hectares of planted vineyard, which was predicted to grow to 9777 hectares by 2006, with sauvignon blanc gaining greater dominance in the region with 61 percent of total plantings, followed by pinot noir and then chardonnay. Riesling and pinot gris are predicted to be the next most planted grapes, lagging a long way behind the others.

'The challenge for New Zealand is to see just how strong the international opportunity is. There are a lot of unanswered questions about where the wine markets will be in the future,' says Nobilo Wine Group chief executive officer, Brian Vieceli.

The other challenge is for those who are passionate about wine to remain true to their goals and to themselves.

Hans and Therese Herzog not only brought their philosophy with them from Switzerland to Marlborough; they moved their entire Michelin-starred restaurant and transplanted it in identical fashion at their little winery called Herzog Wine Collection.

Marlborough wineries

Allan Scott Wines & Estates

Jacksons Road, Blenheim, phone (03) 572 9054

Belmont Wines

221 Paynters Road, Blenheim, phone (03) 577 8082

Cellier Le Brun

Terrace Road, Renwick, phone (03) 572 8859

Charles Wiffen Wines

New Renwick Road, Blenheim, phone (03) 319 2826

Churton

Renwick, Blenheim, phone (03) 572 4007

Clifford Bay Estate

26 Rapaura Road, Blenheim, phone (03) 572 7148

Clos Marguerite

671 Seaview Road, Seddon, phone (03) 575 7721

Cloudy Bay Vineyards

Jacksons Road, Blenheim, phone (03) 520 9140

Domaine Georges Michel

Vintage Lane, Rapaura, phone (03) 572 7230

Fairhall Downs Estate Wines

70 Wrekin Road, Brancott Valley, phone (03) 572 8356

Forrest Estate

Blicks Road, Renwick, phone (03) 572 9084

Foxes Island Wines

Cnr Rapaura Road and State Highway 6, Rapaura,

phone (03) 572 7940

Framingham Wine Company

Condors Bend Road, Renwick, phone (03) 572 8884

Fromm Winery

Godfrey Road, Blenheim, phone (03) 572 9355

Grove Mill Wine Company

Waihopai Valley Road, Renwick, phone (03) 572 8200

Herzog Wine Collection

81 Jeffries Road, Rapaura, phone (03) 572 8770

Highfield Estate

Brookby Road, Blenheim, phone (03) 572 9244

Huia Vineyards

22 Boyces Road, Rapaura, phone (03) 572 8326

Hunter's Wines

Rapaura Road, Blenheim, phone (03) 572 8489

Isabel Estate Vineyard

72 Hawkesbury Road, Renwick, phone (03) 572 8300

Jackson Estate

Jacksons Road, Blenheim, phone (03) 572 8287

Johanneshof Cellars

State Highway 1, Koromiko, phone (03) 573 7035

Lake Chalice Wines

Vintage Lane, Rapaura, phone (03) 572 9327

Lawson's Dry Hills Wines

Alabama Road, Blenheim, phone (03) 578 7674

Le Brun Family Estate

455 Rapaura Road, Blenheim, phone (03) 572 9876

Montana Wines

State Highway 1, Riverlands, Blenheim, phone (03) 578 2099

Mount Riley Wines

Cnr Malthouse Lane and State Highway 1, Blenheim, phone 0800 494 632

Mud House Wine Company

Condors Bend Road, Renwick, phone (03) 572 9490

Old Road Wines

Wynvale, Blenheim, phone (03) 572 8450

Omaka Springs Estates

Kennedys Road, Omaka Valley, phone (03) 572 9933

Provincial Vineyards

Jacksons Road, Blenheim, phone (03) 572 8943

Riverby Estate

Jacksons Road, Blenheim, phone (03) 572 9509

Saint Clair Estate Wines

156 New Renwick Road, Blenheim, phone (03) 578 8695

Seresin Estate

Bedford Road, Renwick, phone (03) 572 9408

Staete Landt Vineyard

275 Rapaura Road, Rapaura, phone (03) 572 9886

Thainstone Winery

Giffords Road, Blenheim, phone (03) 572 8823

Vavasour Wines

Redwood Pass Road, Lower Dashwood, phone (03) 575 7481

Villa Maria Marlborough Winery

Cnr Paynters and New Renwick Road, Blenheim, phone (03) 577 9530

Wairau River Wines

Giffords Road, Blenheim, phone (03) 572 9800

Whitehaven Wine Company

Blicks Road, Renwick, Blenheim, phone (03) 572 7588

Wither Hills Vineyards Marlborough

211 New Renwick Road, Blenheim, phone (03) 578 4036

Waipara and Canterbury

Waipara and Canterbury are geographically close but they are distant relations when it comes to their climate, soils and the styles of wine they produce, as a new wave of Waipara grape planting and winemaking is showing.

'Welcome to the Hurunui' says an unobtrusive road sign, posted alongside State Highway 1 in North Canterbury.

As I drive up out of Christchurch the clouds and rain dissipate, giving way to brilliant sunshine and noticeably warmer temperatures which characterise the region of Waipara in North Canterbury. The area in vines here is small but growing fast, and the region is home to an excitingly diverse range of soils and sites. Although it still retains a sleepy appearance, there is no doubt that the town of Waipara and its wine region are set to boom.

At the time of writing, Montana Wines was soon to plant hundreds of hectares of new vineyards here. A move which Waipara winemakers describe as extremely gratifying because, in the words of one of them, 'it's nice to be endorsed by the big guys'.

For all that, Waipara is still a toddler in winemaking terms. For most of its vinous life, it has lived under the shadow of the Canterbury Plains wine scene. But few wine regions in New Zealand can boast as markedly different climates and geography as Canterbury and Waipara and it is becoming increasingly clear that Waipara rather than Canterbury is home to the most consistent wines from this vinous double-act.

The country's wine industry body, Winegrowers New Zealand, links these two very disparate regions together for the purpose of gathering statistics. But in reality Canterbury and Waipara have little in common, except for their position along the east coast of the South Island.

Waipara is growing in vineyard area; Canterbury is relatively static and, by some people's calculations, set to decline over the next decade. Compared with Waipara's relatively compact area, Canterbury sprawls for some 180 kilometres, from Amberley in the north to near Timaru in the south.

Fly into the region on a sunny autumn day and the pilot is likely to announce that the air temperature on the ground is a cool 5°C, or less, in the South Island's largest city, Christchurch.

The Canterbury Plains flank the city's western side and are at least as cool as the crisp air temperature in the nearby city. The

PREVIOUS PAGES: Pinot noir vines at the tiny Floating Mountain vineyard, owned by Mark and Michelle Rattray, who bought former Cabinet Minister Derek Quigley's vineyard in the late 1980s.
ABOVE: Like most wineries in Waipara, Mountford is minuscule in size but big on quality and owned by a hands-on couple who do all of the marketing, some of the sales and much of the vineyard work too – Michael and Buffy Eaton.
RIGHT: Mountford in autumn captures the colours of the South Island's change of seasons.

rainfall here tends to be low but cooling sea breezes mean that, in a relatively cold year, many of the grapes do not benefit from enough growing degree days to bring them to total ripeness.

Waipara is about an hour's drive north of Christchurch and the air is distinctively warmer and drier. As well as being an altogether more pleasant place to sit in the sun and while away an hour or two with a glass of wine, it is far better suited to growing grapes.

The rainfall in Waipara is even lower than on the Plains, while the growing degree days measured by the meteorological station are much higher and frosts are fewer, but not insignificant.

As Chris Donaldson of Pegasus Bay winery says, Waipara is less susceptible to frost than Canterbury but frost is an issue for both regions. 'It's just a matter of getting out of bed to put the wind machines on, if there is an early frost or any other type of frost, and sometimes they can hit even in early spring – it is not usual but it does happen.'

Waipara is well protected by the Teviotdale Hills from the cool easterly winds that blow their way onto the Canterbury coastline, which makes many parts of the Canterbury Plains relatively marginal for grape-growing. Waipara's heat summation is about the same as Marlborough, in terms of the length of the growing season, with about 1150 to 1250 growing degree days.

Waipara's soils vary from silt to stony alluvial soils near the Waipara River to chalky clay loams, often rich in limestone, on the hillsides. The Canterbury Plains, braided with four major rivers, are mainly shallow, stony and fast-draining.

At the time of writing, Canterbury and Waipara combined was New Zealand's sixth largest wine region with 517 hectares of vines planted. Predictions for the future show this region will again be in the top five by 2005, if not earlier.

A rash of vine planting took place in Canterbury and Waipara in the late 1970s and early 1980s. Most of the winemakers involved at that time are still in the region today.

The most dynamic growth has occurred very recently. Waipara is predicted to have experienced at least a 50 percent increase in its vineyard area between 2002 and 2005, most significantly by the country's largest winery, Montana Wines, which has planted a 160

hectare block, the Camshorn Vineyard near Waipara, with riesling, pinot gris and pinot noir. Montana also inherited 53 hectares of Corbans' Omihi vineyard when it purchased Corbans Wines in November 2000.

When Montana took over the Omihi vineyard, there were just five hectares of 20-year-old riesling vines planted with the balance of the area being new vines. Unusually for a New Zealand vineyard, this one was planted with relatively narrow spacing between the vines, which were only two metres apart instead of the usual three metre spacing. This is thought to result in lower yields for each vine, in tandem with improved, more intense flavour and better potential for full ripening.

In 20 years' time, Mountford Vineyard winemaker Chung Pin ('CP') Lin predicts, Canterbury as a wine region will be virtually non-existent while Waipara will be even bigger.

'Waipara is growing by the day with new vineyard plantings and its quality is on a steady upward climb today, even as we speak,' says the winemaker confidently.

Not everybody agrees.

'After observing the evolution of Canterbury and the rest of the South Island for the past 30 years I find it amusing to hear anybody predict the demise of certain areas of Canterbury as opposed to Waipara.' Danny Schuster

Veteran viticulturist and winemaker Daniel Schuster, who began growing grapes in the region 30 years ago, now makes all of his wines predominantly from Waipara-grown grapes. He says the final viticultural map for Canterbury and Waipara is still a long way off.

'There can be no doubt that the various districts will continue to specialise further as is happening elsewhere in New Zealand. Which area will prevail will not depend on fashion but on the consistency of wines made and the marketing efforts surrounding those wines.'

The first grapes were planted in Canterbury by a group of French settlers, who arrived at Akaroa on Banks Peninsula in 1840 and planted vine cuttings from which they made wine for their own consumption. There are still several small vineyards on Banks Peninsula but they make up a mere trickle of the wine produced in the wider region. The peninsula tends to be wetter and slightly warmer than the Canterbury Plains and also hillier.

LEFT: Jane and Michael East have long had a passion for wine, which they turned into reality by establishing Muddy Water winery in Waipara in the late 1990s. Today their winemaker, Belinda Gould, harnesses unbelievably good flavours from their vineyard's pinotage and syrah as well as the region's two strong points: riesling and pinot noir.
ABOVE: Danny Schuster is nothing if not an international commodity. He was born in Czechoslovakia, trained in winemaking and viticulture in Germany and has now lived in New Zealand for decades while travelling annually to Italy and the United States where he works as a viticultural consultant. His original take on Marlborough sauvignon blanc is now highly sought after by Europeans keen on a different flavour in their wine glass.

In the mid-twentieth century, a small vineyard was established by W.H. Meyers near Sumner Beach in Christchurch. It was not a successful venture and the vines were uprooted in 1949.

Viticulture in the Canterbury region remained static until the mid-1970s when an experimental half hectare vineyard was planted in several grape varieties under the auspices of Lincoln College. The first commercial planting of grapes in Canterbury was at Belfast (at Turners Orchard) in 1977 when about four hectares of pinot gris, pinot noir, gewürztraminer and riesling were planted for the Cathedral winery, which was sold to Ernie Hunter in 1981 and later became the source for the first Hunter's wines in 1982. Hunter later moved to Marlborough but continued to use Canterbury grown grapes until the mid-1980s.

Canterbury's first commercial winery, St Helena, was established in 1978 by Robin and Norman Mundy at Belfast. The winery's first commercial vintage was 1981, from which only two white wines were made. The first red, a pinot noir, was made in 1982 by Daniel Schuster; this wine became highly acclaimed after winning a gold medal at a national wine competition and was still drinking well in 2003, according to some of the region's fussiest winemakers.

Canterbury wine pioneer Ivan Donaldson planted a fruit salad of grapes in 1976 on a tiny vineyard on the Canterbury Plains, from which he made pinot noir, riesling, müller-thurgau, gewürztraminer, pinot meunier, chardonnay and cabernet sauvignon. Also made was what he and others involved had thought to be merlot but after a few years realised it was actually chenin blanc.

Donaldson says it was not a particularly good wine but this hobby venture (none of the wines made were sold commercially) proved to him that there was potential to make top quality wine somewhere within the region.

'I made my first wine in Canterbury in 1967, which was from the albany surprise grape variety and we thought that this new wine was great to drink but it was obviously nothing compared to the quality that we have today.'

Ivan Donaldson decided to grow grapes in Waipara rather than Canterbury because of its relatively warmer climate and in 1985 he planted grapes for a vine nursery at what is today the Pegasus Bay winery in Waipara. The following year he planted his vineyard there. Today Ivan and his wife Chris have been joined in the winery by two of their four sons.

The oldest, Matthew, is the winemaker, along with his partner, Lynette Hudson. And Edward (Ed to his friends) is the marketing man at the winery.

LEFT: Netted grapevines at Muddy Water vineyard just prior to harvesting will prove, once again, that Waipara has the potential to produce top-quality wine, despite the region's thwarted start in the 1960s, when John McCaskey of Glenmark winery was flooded out.
ABOVE: Pinot noir, riesling, chardonnay and sauvignon blanc are the most widely planted grape varieties in the Waipara region today. Pegasus Bay winery has a relatively long track record with producing impressive pinot noir and now other wineries are proving it to be the best-suited red grape to this cool-climate wine region. Newcomers hope that syrah might equal the success of pinot noir in Waipara.

'I always thought they might follow their father into his first choice of career, medicine,' says Chris Donaldson, with a bit of a laugh, adding that her sons always perceived helping their dad out with wine stuff to be a bit tedious.

'Now they are all passionate about wine and our two sons who are not working directly with it are feeling left out and thinking about coming home to follow suit.'

Donaldson says there are pockets of potential for growing grapes on the Canterbury Plains, like the Burnham area. 'I have tasted first class grapes – pinot noir, chardonnay, riesling and sauvignon blanc – out of this area, but it is about finding the right little microclimate.'

In Waipara, grapes were first planted in 1965 by John McCaskey. Luck was not on his side at the time and a flood and bad vineyard site put paid to any ideas of grape-growing until 1981 when he planted on a more suitable site. His first wines under the Glenmark label flowed in 1986. Around this time, Waipara began to grow as Daniel Schuster and the Donaldsons planted grapes. They were followed by others.

In October 2003, Montana Wines started planting the region's largest and newest vineyards.

Pinot noir is the most widely planted grape in Waipara and is set to stay that way, even with the massive new vineyards that are scheduled to be planted. After pinot noir, chardonnay is the most planted grape variety, followed by sauvignon blanc and riesling and small plantings of pinot gris.

There are also very tiny quantities of merlot, cabernet sauvignon, cabernet franc, syrah and a little gewürztraminer, which winemaker Theo Coles says does best in Akaroa.

'Most people think that Akaroa has little or nothing to offer us in terms of grapes for winemaking,' says Coles, 'but the truth is that its potential just keeps being screwed up. The soils there are heavily volcanic and that absolutely does not suit some grapes. But for gewürztraminer it seems to be just about perfect and I see huge potential there.'

The New Zealand Grape and Wine Industry Statistical Annual predicts that by 2005 vineyards on the Canterbury Plains and in Waipara will be planted mainly in pinot noir and pinot gris.

'You get one bite at the market and you form your reputation on that. Let that market down and you are gone,' says winemaker, viticulturist (and world cactus expert), Danny Schuster.

When Schuster was working in Australia in 1970 he was asked by viticulturist Joe Corban what he thought of New Zealand wines.

ABOVE: Nigel Green, assistant vineyard manager at Giesen's Burnham vineyard on the Canterbury Plains.
RIGHT: The Giesen brothers began their medium-sized winery in Canterbury but today they have shifted much of their operation north to Marlborough, utilising the best grapes their existing vineyards in this region provide.

'I said I thought New Zealand wines were not good but that they tasted like they had the potential to be great,' says Schuster, 'and then I asked where exactly New Zealand was.'

By 1972, the Prague-born Schuster had been to South Africa and France to make wine and then moved to Christchurch. Alongside a small group of other winemakers-to-be, he began experimenting with growing different grape varieties.

Schuster has been in New Zealand more or less since then. More because he eventually married a New Zealander and established a vineyard; less because he still works as a roving viticultural expert, working for parts of each year in Tuscany and California.

In the mid-1970s Schuster worked for Montana Wines in Marlborough, before moving back to Canterbury to work at the new St Helena winery until the mid-1980s when he set up his own vineyard at Omihi, specialising in pinot noir. He established his vineyard at exactly the same time as Pegasus Bay's vineyard was being set up, just down the road.

'I wanted to focus only on pinot noir rather than being distracted by other varieties,' says Schuster, who planted his grapevines closer than usual in order to reap the rewards of high density planting, which result in more concentrated flavours from vines that have to work harder than if they were planted further apart.

Today Schuster makes what has grown to become one of New Zealand's most impressive pinot noirs from this close planted Omihi Hills vineyard. He also makes a top quality chardonnay to match, from grapes grown at the Petrie vineyard in southern Canterbury, and he makes one of the country's best sauvignon blancs.

It is an unusual wine, made in tiny quantities at his little winery, which is tucked into one of the many folds in the Omihi Hills. The grapes he uses to make this sauvignon blanc, named Mt Nelson, come from several growers in Marlborough and the wine is sold mainly to the European wine market, with just a smattering of bottles making their way into some of New Zealand's best restaurants and wine stores.

The European connection of most importance for Waipara is winemaker Louis Barruol, who comes from the oldest winery in Gigondas, France – Chateau de Saint Cosme.

In one breath, Barruol says he doesn't know how to be a commercial winemaker and in another explains that his wines, most of which cost less than $20, are made to be drunk as soon as you buy them and are exported to 35 countries.

'I always prefer a cheap wine which says something rather than a very ambitious wine which says nothing – and you get plenty of that,' says the outspoken Frenchman.

In 2003, he was visiting New Zealand to start a winery (as yet unnamed) in Waipara in partnership with Waipara winemaker Theo Coles, who works as assistant winemaker at Daniel Schuster Wines.

Together they have purchased about 40 hectares of land in Waipara, which they plan to plant with syrah, viognier and roussanne grapes. Suggest it is relatively cool in Waipara for these supposedly heat-loving vines, traditionally grown in the Rhône Valley, France, and Barruol insists that this climate is exactly the sort in which the grapes do well.

Theo Coles adds quickly that pinot noir will also be made.

Coles expects that the first vintage to be made from contract grown grapes from 2002, but it will be at least another five years before their own grapes are ready for winemaking. As Barruol says, making wine from young vines is like asking a child to run 100 metres in 10 seconds.

'It's too stressful for the vines and in the long term it also ruins the balance of the vineyard.' Besides, many of their vines will not be planted until 2005.

'We will be very high-end focused,' says Coles. 'There is no point in being average when you are growing something that is marginal in terms of climate, and we are well aware that syrah is not going to be ripe in this region until probably about the end of May.' All of this makes the new winery both exciting and relatively risky. Time and taste will tell, but Barruol's own wines are of a uniformly high standard at all of their different prices, and Coles' work at Daniel Schuster Wines is also well respected, which bodes well for them.

Not all Canterbury tales are as exotic as those of Schuster and Barruol.

Jane and Michael East, who own Muddy Water Fine Wines, work hard at their highly regarded winery. Jane does the marketing and sales work while Mike works full-time as an obstetrician. It was after tasting one of Waipara winemaker Mark Rattray's first pinot noirs in the late 1980s that the couple knew it was just a matter of time before they tried to make their own wine from grapes grown in the Waipara region.

ABOVE: Pinot noir – here dribbling from the basketpress – is the beginning, middle and end of Daniel Schuster Fine Wines. Grapes are treated with the maximum respect and gentlest possible handling.
RIGHT: Theo Coles, assistant winemaker, operating the basketpress at Daniel Schuster's winery in Omihi, Waipara. The press is gentle on grapes but is labour intensive.

'Mike spoke to a patient who was a land agent one day and said, "If you ever hear about any land up there, let me know".'

Three weeks later they purchased 65 acres of land.

'It was totally unplanned but the site was so good and we now own 100 acres, about a third of which is planted in grapes.'

East says they did not even consider the possibility of planting grapes on the Canterbury Plains. It was clear, she says, where to plant grapes, just not so obvious which ones to plant. In 1993, when they put their first vines in the ground, the vineyard was a fruit salad of everything from pinot noir, chardonnay, riesling and sauvignon blanc to pinotage, syrah, cabernet sauvignon, cabernet franc, merlot and sangiovese.

'We planted a trial block of all those reds because New Zealand was full of people saying "You can't grow all those grapes there" and we just wanted to try.'

Like most Waipara wineries they had settled on pinot noir, chardonnay and riesling as their key varieties.

'The first year we grew sangiovese it was fantastic and after that it hung there and we just could not get it to ripen, so it became clear that it was a no-go,' says East.

'Our cabernets were only a tiny volume and we decided there was a better market for well-made pinotage and syrah from this region but they are a small part of our overall production.'

They then top-grafted pinot noir onto their sauvignon blanc vines because international markets are mainly interested in Marlborough sauvignon blancs, according to East.

'Our riesling has the potential to be better quality in Waipara than sauvignon blanc anyway, so we decided to play to our strengths.'

In 2002, Muddy Water's winemaker Belinda Gould made the first Muddy Water Riesling Unplugged. The dessert styled riesling was made from botrytised grapes, which are relatively unusual in a region as dry as Waipara where the damp conditions necessary to form the botrytis mould on grapes is rare.

Gould made the wine in a late harvest sweet style rather than fully botrytised and unctuously rich. It is sealed with a screw cap.

'We're not doing corks any more,' says Gould, who started at Muddy Water Fine Wines in 1997.

'Apart from our export markets in Germany and the United Kingdom, who still want corks, we have moved totally to the screw cap seal for all of our wines.'

The impetus for this bold move came from an experience at the 2002 Central Otago Pinot Noir Celebration where Gould and East opened 15 bottles of their pinot noir wine.

ABOVE: Belinda Gould, Muddy Water winemaker, is an ardent supporter of screw cap seals for wine, believing that they preserve it just the way it was intended to be as it leaves the winery.
RIGHT: Winemaker notes on a stainless steel tank at Mountford winery, which is housed in an old shipping container, built into a hillside in Waipara.
FAR RIGHT: Mark Rattray is one of the region's most experienced winemakers and as passionate about white grapes as he is about the ubiquitous pinot noir. Rattray is a pioneer in New Zealand of the German grape, scheurebe, often known as scheu and a cross of sylvaner and riesling.

One of the biggest strengths of Waipara and Canterbury is their aromatic white wine grape varieties, some of which are extremely fashionable and others most definitely not, but I believe they are part of our future as much as pinot noir.   Mark Rattray

'Only ten of the wines tasted any good, but only one wine was actually corked. The other four faulty wines were compromised in some way or other, such as oxidation which was quite clearly due to the cork,' says Gould.

Now that riesling, chardonnay and pinot noir at Muddy Water Fine Wines are all sealed with screw caps, the wines are now bottled . with less of the preservative, sulphur dioxide, which is present in all wines globally.

'Because the fruit flavour is so well preserved under a screw cap seal I don't need to use as much sulphur dioxide,' explains Gould. 'The wine matures under a screw cap seal but it does so in a slow, predictable way. With a cork you never know what you're getting, besides which there are good corks and bad corks.'

Floating Mountain, also known by its Maori name of Maukutere, is another evocatively named winery just five minutes' walk from Muddy Water Fine Wines. One of the region's smallest wineries, it is owned by Mark and Michelle Rattray.

'When we came from working for Montana Wines in Auckland to Canterbury, we were actually looking for land in Marlborough but this property became available in 1989 so I bought it,' says Mark Rattray.

Due to his reputation for producing top quality pinot noir from Waipara-grown grapes, Rattray has stayed there, gradually reducing the land he owned from an original 36.5 hectares to 11 hectares today, of which just 1.6 hectares is planted in grapes.

'It was just good luck that brought me to Waipara instead of Canterbury,' says Rattray, with a wry smile. 'Very good luck.'

Like all of his winemaking neighbours, he focuses on pinot noir and chardonnay but he also makes a little sauvignon blanc and has planted some scheurebe (also known as scheu, an early twentieth century crossing of silvaner and riesling); the first grapes of this German variety came from the 2003 vintage.

'I am looking for flavours of grapefruit and blackcurrant from this variety. I can make some wonderful stickies with it, but we haven't got a big enough area planted to make a lot, so I will probably make a sort of spatlese, medium dry style while we discover what sort of taste we can generate in the grape in this region.'

Black Estate, Bell Hill, Daniel Schuster Fine Wines and Mountford Estate are all highly respected Waipara wineries, which have shown the best potential for making top pinot noirs.

The most established of these tiny Waipara wineries is Michael and Buffy Eaton's Mountford Estate, a cleverly concealed winery at the top of a majestic slope planted in pinot noir and chardonnay.

'Our first night in Waipara was in a tent by the Omihi Stream before we had paid for the land,' says Michael. 'An electric fence encircled the paddock we were in to stop our horses coming in.'

The name is an amalgamation of the Mount (Mount Cass) that presides over the top of their 198 hectares and the ford through the trickle that is Omihi Stream at the entrance to their property.

Initially the couple planted four hectares in front of their home, divided equally between pinot noir and chardonnay. Now they have planted a further two hectares on the steep slope behind the winery in pinot noir and pinot gris.

Waipara Springs, one of the Waipara's most established wineries, was founded in 1990. It is owned and run by the Moore and Grant families. Wines produced include chardonnay, sauvignon blanc, riesling, pinot noir, cabernet sauvignon and merlot. Despite this wide range it is, predictably, the pinot noir and riesling that are of the most consistently high standard, reflecting what appears to be at least two out of three of the region's biggest viticultural strengths.

The other emerging strength of the Canterbury and Waipara regions, viticulturally, is chardonnay. And the emerging style is less about fruitiness and more about a kind of clean, fresh and hard to define complexity, derived from leaving the fermented grapejuice on

its yeast lees for longer than has traditionally been the case in this country's young wine history.

Daniel Schuster, Matthew Donaldson and Lynette Hudson are proponents of this and their wines are all the better for it: more grown-up stylistically and far more drinkable than tutti-fruity Kiwi chardonnay can sometimes be.

Pegasus Bay Winery has about 45 hectares of grapes planted and also an experimental vine nursery, on which different clones of pinot noir are trialled on several different rootstocks, in a quest to find what works best. This is a complex exercise and findings are not yet conclusive, but this type of meticulous research will yield results that are of enormous importance not only to this winery but to the whole of the region and to the New Zealand wine industry.

Grapes are also sourced from contract grape-growers around the South Island, from which Pegasus Bay's Main Divide range is made. While Main Divide wines are lower in price than most of those under the better known Pegasus Bay label, the wines are not so much a second tier as an entirely different range. In a sense, these are what the wine industry terms 'entry level' wines but at $25-ish, the Main Divide pinot noir is hardly an everyday wine for most drinkers. It is, however, better than ever since Ivan Donaldson now spends a significant amount of time sourcing grapes from which to make wine under this banner.

While pinot noir is Pegasus Bay's most delicious, important, best-known commodity, cabernet-based red wines are also made here.

'It's a pretty labour-intensive thing to do, making cabernet, and we will probably focus the wine on being predominantly merlot from the 2003 vintage onwards, but we enjoy making it and getting it ripe in this climate,' says Ivan Donaldson.

Winemakers here planted a quirky assortment of red grapes to add into this blend in the early 2000s, which included both malbec and syrah.

For Waipara winemaker Alan McCorkindale, it was the limestone soil and north facing aspect that led him to Waipara. That, and the riesling grapes he had been sourcing from Waipara since 1989 in his role as winemaker at Corbans' Marlborough winery. When he finished there, in 1997, he moved to Waipara to make wine for himself.

Ask him which grapes will do best in Waipara in the future and McCorkindale is sage. 'That's a hard one. This year, 2003, we picked the best sauvignon blancs that I've ever made for anybody. Sparkling

wine is what we really had in mind but that's very slow to make so we need something else as well.'

His 'something else' includes aromatic grapes: gewürztraminer, pinot gris and sauvignon blanc. And although he does not use grapes grown on the Canterbury Plains, McCorkindale says he regularly tastes 'very impressive rieslings made with grapes grown there'.

One of the region's newest winemakers is Mike Wersing, who has established Pyramid Valley Wines in Waipara. In 2003 he had not yet released any wines but other winemakers in the region had high hopes for Wersing's contribution, especially his pending pinot noir.

One sip of riesling tells the story of two distinctive wine regions when the wine is made by ex-pat Australian winemaker Kym Rayner of Torlesse Wines.

Rayner's dry riesling is made from grapes grown in Waipara; his sweeter version is made with Canterbury-grown grapes.

'The reason is simple: without the residual sugar [the grape sugar left over when a fermentation has been stopped], the Canterbury wine would be unbalanced,' explains Rayner. And he likes rieslings with a little residual sugar. As he says, there is a lot to recommend that style of wine. Yet it is his Waipara riesling, a wine that is all limes and spice in taste, that really does it for most riesling lovers. This sort

'You don't have to be Einstein to work out that Waipara is a great location in terms of marketing advantages. And it also happens to be a great place to grow grapes.'

Chris Donaldson, Pegasus Bay Winery

of almost bone-dry riesling is the style of wine that heralds the future of the Waipara region. It has elegance, intensity and balance that hint at the potential greatness of whites from this region.

Like many Waipara winemakers, Rayner and other shareholders in Torlesse Wines established their winery in 1991 at West Melton, on the Canterbury Plains. But when he started working on a Waipara vineyard and found the climate to be significantly warmer, he then decided to shift the whole operation there.

There is plenty to attract winemakers and wine drinkers to what is happening on the Canterbury Plains, but there is stronger potential in Waipara. And as Waipara's vineyards get older, the style of wines made from grapes here will evolve. Sub-regions within Waipara will become distinctive not only in the vineyards but also in that most important place, where it really counts: the wine drinker's glass.

ABOVE: Waipara's grape-growing climate is similar to Marlborough's, judging by heat and rainfall, but there is a far greater diurnal fluctuation (the difference in temperature between day and night).

Waipara and Canterbury wineries

Alan McCorkindale

Omihi Road, Waipara, North Canterbury, phone 0800 423 532

Bell Hill Vineyard

105 Old Weka Pass Road, Waikari, North Canterbury, phone (03) 379 4374

Bentwood Wines

634-1229 Akaroa Highway, Tai Tapu, Canterbury, phone (03) 329 6191

Black Estate Wines

614 Omihi Road, RD 3, Amberley, North Canterbury, phone (03) 314 5888

Canterbury House Winery

780 Glasnevin Road, State Highway 1, Waipara, North Canterbury,
phone (03) 314 6900

Charles Wiffen Wines

1639 Parnassus Road, Cheviot, Canterbury, phone (03) 319 2826

Daniel Schuster Wines

192 Reeces Road, Omihi, North Canterbury, phone (03) 314 5901

Darjon Vineyard

North Eyre Road, Swannanoa, North Canterbury, phone (03) 312 6045

Dry Plains Fine Wines

Two Chain Road, Burnham, Central Canterbury, phone (03) 981 9224

Ellesmere Wine Company

Days Road, RD 4, Christchurch, phone (03) 329 5311

Fiddler's Green Wines

Georges Road, Waipara, North Canterbury, phone (03) 314 6979

Floating Mountain Winery

418 Omihi Road, Waipara, North Canterbury, phone (03) 314 6710

French Farm Vineyards

French Farm Valley Road, RD 2, Akaroa, Canterbury, phone (03) 304 5784

Gatehouse Wines

Jowers Road, RD 6, West Melton, Canterbury, phone (03) 342 9682

Giesen Wine Estate

Burnham School Road, RD 5, Canterbury, phone (03) 347 6729

Glenmark Wines

RD 3, Amberley, North Canterbury, phone (03) 314 6828

Horsford Downs

360 Quarry Road, Whiterock, RD 2, Rangiora, North Canterbury

Kaituna Valley

230 Kaituna Valley Road, RD 2, Christchurch, phone (03) 329 0110

Larcomb Vineyard

Cnr Main South Road & Larcombs Road, Rolleston, Canterbury,
phone (03) 347 8909

Melness Wines

1816 Main Road, Cust Village, North Canterbury, phone (03) 312 5402

Morworth Estate Vineyard

Block Road, RD 6, Canterbury, phone (03) 349 5014

Mount Cass (aka Alpine Pacific Wine Company)

133 Mt Cass Road, Waipara, North Canterbury, phone (03) 314 6834

Mountford Vineyard

434 Omihi Road, Waipara, North Canterbury, phone (03) 314 6819

Muddy Water Winery

424 Omihi Road, Waipara, North Canterbury, phone (03) 314 6966

Pegasus Bay Winery

Stockgrove Road, Waipara, North Canterbury, phone (03) 314 6869

Rossendale Winery

168 Old Tai Tapu Road, Christchurch, phone (03) 322 7780

St Helena Wine Estate

259 Coutts Island Road, Belfast, Christchurch, phone (03) 323 8202

Sandihurst Wines

Main West Coast Road, West Melton, Canterbury, phone (03) 347 8289

Sherwood Estate Wines

Church Road, Waipara, North Canterbury, phone (03) 314 6962

Sirocco Wines

111 Methven Barhill Road, Rakaia, Central Canterbury, phone (03) 302 7252

Swannanoa Wines

Jowers Road (off West Coast Road), West Melton, Canterbury,
phone (03) 342 9682

Takamatua Valley Vineyards

59 Long Bay Road, Takamatua, Akaroa, Canterbury, phone (03) 304 8990

Torlesse Wines

Loffhagen Drive, Waipara, North Canterbury, phone (03) 314 6929

Trent's Estate

Trent's Road, Templeton, RD 6, Christchurch, phone (03) 349 6940

Waipara Downs

Bains Road, RD 3, Amberley, North Canterbury, phone (03) 314 6873

Waipara Hills Wine Estate

20A Connaught Drive, Hornby, Christchurch, phone (03) 344 5052

Waipara Springs Winery

409 Omihi Road, State Highway 1, Waipara, North Canterbury,
phone (03) 314 6777

Waipara West

376 Ram Paddock Road, Amberley, North Canterbury, phone (03) 314 8699

Wattlebank

150 Old Tai Tapu Road, Christchurch, phone (03) 322 9071

Whiterock Vineyards

360 Quarry Road, Whiterock, RD 2, Rangiora, North Canterbury,
phone (03) 312 8711

Central Otago

Central Otago has morphed from being the butt of jokes about marginal climates in which to grow grapes to being one of New Zealand's fastest growing wine regions. Central is home to some of this country's most individual tasting pinot noirs, rieslings and pinot gris. The inimitable style and growing quantity of these edgy southern wines is as much a source of debate as it is of pleasure. But with a large proportion of land now planted in grapes, the region's winemakers are here to stay for the long haul and they are confident about their future and that of their wines.

Ever since wine has been made in Central Otago in modern times, it has been described as edgy, herby and tasting of wild thyme flavours; light in body and substance. Sometimes this is complimentary but more often than not it is a way of dismissing the region's attempts at winemaking. In the first few years of this decade, many writers, winemakers and others within the New Zealand wine industry have begun to sit up and take notice of the new wave of wines that are being created from grapes grown here, in the world's southernmost wine producing region.

Change started kicking in about 1996, when Central's wine industry jumped onto a roller-coaster ride of furiously speedy growth, a track it is still zooming along. That year the number of grapevines planted in the region doubled from 46 to 92 hectares.

Then, in 1997, it grew again, this time from 92 to 135 hectares and in 1998 that figure exploded to 210 hectares. The fastest and most significant growth has been this millennium and the region now boasts over 800 – and growing – hectares of grapevines.

Not only is Central one of the most spectacularly beautiful places on the planet, it is also unique in New Zealand viticultural terms, being the only inland grape-growing area in this country as well as being the only place where the vines are thoroughly doused in snow and ice each winter.

Grapes were first planted in this region when the southern gold rush was in full swing, in the 1860s. Modern winemaking in Otago was pioneered in the 1970s but the biggest growth has been in the last five years, during which Central has gone from seventh place to being the fourth biggest wine region in the country.

PREVIOUS PAGES: The Remarkables mountain range flanking the western side of Queenstown could not be more aptly named but it is not strictly in the Central Otago region.
ABOVE: Like all grapevines in Central Otago, these ones at Chard Farm begin to bud and flower later than anywhere else in New Zealand, due to their southerly location.
RIGHT: Soils in Central Otago tend to be the driest in New Zealand, as evidenced in this arid-looking vineyard that belongs to Gibbston Valley Wines.

The phenomenal growth in grape plantings in the last half decade has changed not only the size of this once-tiny winemaking area, but also the nature of the wines made here.

Central's best and worst wines often taste herbal and can be light-bodied. What separates many of the top wines from the others is that they encapsulate big fruit flavours, amalgamated with those inimitable wild thyme flavours; the same as the aromas you can smell in the wind on hot summer days down here.

Rather than remaining within the cooler climates of the Gibbston Valley, Wanaka and Alexandra, the predominant grape-growing areas till recently, winemakers are spreading their viticultural wings in almost every direction in search of warmer zones.

The country's highest altitude vines are now planted on the shores of the small and unrealistically glassy Lake Hayes. This cool area is suitable only for making sparkling wine, according to wine-maker Jeff Sinnott, who works at Amisfield winery on the shores of the lake.

New vineyards are also sprouting slightly further south in a mix of soils and rocky areas in the Earnscleugh Basin by Alexandra and north to Omarama.

Most significant are new vineyards in the Cromwell Basin, which incorporates Bannockburn, Lowburn, Northburn, Bendigo and other pieces of land deemed suitable or worth trialling for viticulture in the Basin. It is here, in the midst of all these Scottish settler names, that pinot noir has found its most consistent expression in Central Otago.

Wine is the new gold in Central. And like the region's first gold rush in the 1860s, people are searching with frightening fervour for sub-regions within the area, in which to exploit the highly sought after commodity that is pinot noir.

ABOVE: The soil strata at the relatively new Carrick winery in Bannockburn reveals that hard bedrock makes up most of the top layer.
RIGHT: Gibbston Valley was the first winery in the region to create an underground barrel hall, which attracts thousands of visitors every year.

Wines made from grapes grown in the Cromwell Basin taste starkly different to the region's other wines. The sub-regions in the Cromwell Basin have one feature in common: the ability to ripen grapes more consistently than anywhere else in Central. But more new – and suitable – pockets of land are being discovered.

In 2004, pinot noir occupied more than 70 percent of Central's total vineyard area, followed by chardonnay, pinot gris, riesling and sauvignon blanc – which occupies only a tiny portion of vineyard land. Other grapes grown here include gewürztraminer, merlot, pinotage, syrah and, in particularly small quantities, breidecker, müller-thurgau,

sémillon, blauberger and cabernet sauvignon. The *New Zealand Wine and Grape Industry Statistical Annual* predicts that pinot noir will remain the dominant grape variety in the region and this will be followed by pinot gris, chardonnay and riesling.

What characterises Central, even more than the dramatic snow and ice in winter, is the joint ownership nature of many wineries and the relatively recent large foreign investment.

Two of the four biggest wineries in the region are owned in part by those who grow the grapes. That means several people with hefty chunks of land allow a winery to contract-grow their grapes and have a long term relationship with that winery.

This way, a talented but otherwise undercapitalised winemaker and winemaking team has consistent access to grapes from good vineyards without having to invest in planting and establishing all of their vineyards.

Another reason Central Otago has experienced such mammoth vineyard growth in a relatively short time is the injection of capital from overseas.

'Money from further afield than New Zealand is one of the biggest changes in the region in the last few years and it comes mainly from the wine industry in the United States,' says Grant Taylor, winemaker at Gibbston Valley winery. 'People have come for the fishing and love it and want to invest, or winemakers have come here for a vintage and it's had a snowball effect.'

Taylor says that those investing significant sums of money in vineyards in this region do not do it because they want to make mediocre wines. 'They don't just want to play. They have tasted enough to think it's worthwhile economically for the global wine industry to invest money here.'

Those who have access to good grapes in Central Otago every single year will be able to wow the world with a red wine that is as distinctive, unusual and powerful as New Zealand's best sauvignon blancs. Gone are the jokes about marginal climates for growing grapes; Central is now home to some of New Zealand's most celebrated pinot noirs.

Just 31 years after the first grapevines were planted in Central Otago, the region was proclaimed one of three most suitable areas in New Zealand in which to grow grapes.

The glowing decree came in 1895 from government viticulturist Romeo Bragato, on loan from the Australian government, who toured New Zealand to assess the country's suitability for grape growing for the purposes of making wine.

His tour began at the unlikely location of Bluff in Southland and the first glass of New Zealand wine he tasted was in Arrowtown, Central Otago.

Bragato, a Dalmatian born, Italian trained graduate in viticulture and winemaking, said that there were few areas in New Zealand not suitable for high quality grape-growing and winemaking. Bragato's enthusiasm was so contagious it resulted in the establishment of the Central Otago Vine and Fruitgrowers' Association. Unfortunately, the word 'vine' was dropped from the title and it took until the 1950s for Bragato's pronouncement to be vindicated. His influence permeates modern viticulture in New Zealand so much today that the annual grape-growers' conference is named after him.

The region's first vines were planted by Frenchman Jean Desire Feraud, who planted vines in 1864 near Clyde. Ironically his red wine, named 'burgundy', won a prize at a wine competition in Sydney in 1881. It is unlikely that the wine was made from the pinot noir grape but its success is uncanny in light of the focus in the region on pinot noir today.

'Central's best pinot noirs have a wow factor that no other red wine in New Zealand has yet conjured up.'   Steve Smith, shareholder in Central Otago's Peregrine Wines

Central's wine industry then lapsed for 90-odd years, until the 1970s and 1980s when modern pioneers established vineyards and later set up wineries in the region. The enterprising late Rolfe Mills (Rippon Vineyard), Bill Grant ((William Hill Vineyard), Alan Brady (founder of Gibbston Valley and now at Mt Edward winery, also his own) and Verdun Burgess and Sue Edwards (Black Ridge) all helped to shape the face of the modern Central Otago wine industry, as did numerous others.

The first wine made from Central Otago-grown grapes was produced at the Te Kauwhata viticultural research station in the Waikato, in 1985, when grapes were air-freighted north specially for the job. In 1987, grapes were crushed at the small Taramea winery, which is no longer in existence. Winemaking facilities have been thin on the ground, so that winemakers have utilised everything from a mobile bottling plant to a large cooperative wine crushing facility and winery as well as the winery facilities of friends and contacts in the industry. Winemakers predict that as the massive new vineyards begin producing grapes in the next five years, there will be enormous pressure on existing wineries to crush and process grapes from other, winery-less ventures.

Ever since actor Sam Neill produced a pinot noir from his tiny Two Paddocks vineyard in Central Otago, the region has developed the kudos that is the envy of all other wine regions in New Zealand – whether or not winemakers admit to it. Neill was born and bred in Dunedin, four hours away, and as the son of a wine importer was brought up in a wine savvy household. His first wine, released in 1997, tasted promisingly pinot noir-like though very light in style, as is the way with young pinot noir vines. For years, Neill had been impressed with Central's best pinot noirs, and the area was 'like a spiritual home' to him, he said just after his first wine release.

Like Neill, many who own wineries in Central Otago today only live there for part of the year and leave their winemakers in charge of running the show. Quite a few have come from further afield, especially from the United States, to invest money in the region's wineries or move there themselves.

When you drive through the Kawarau Gorge that links Queenstown with the Cromwell Basin, you immediately drop down 200 metres in altitude and hit the valley floor of what may one day be deemed home to New Zealand's best pinot noir grapes. Some say they are that good already but only time, vine age, winemaker experience and a decade or more of vintage variability will determine whether

LEFT: Lake Hayes Vineyard grows a small number of chardonnay and pinot noir vines, which experience very cool growing conditions on the shores of the glassy clear Lake Hayes. Most of this winery's vineyards are situated in the far warmer Cromwell Basin area, an hour's drive away.
BELOW: Central Otago is at 45 degrees south latitude, making it the world's most southern wine-growing region and it is also relatively high, ranging from 200 to 400 metres above sea level. Both factors mean its vines experience the coldest growing conditions in the country, especially in autumn and winter.

this the area of Central that receives the most heat, can consistently make some of the country's best pinot noirs.

It already grows some of the best-tasting apricots in the world, an undisputed fact among fruit lovers who have tried them. And now it offers more pinot noir grapes than most people in the New Zealand wine industry ever would have predicted.

'If you want to make internationally competitive table wines with pinot noir, this is where we need to grow grapes, or in the Earnscleugh Basin by Alexandra,' says winemaker Jeff Sinnott.

When interviewed, Sinnott had been living in Central for less than a year but was an ardent fan of the region's unique expression of pinot noir and its ability to make what he considers to be the best bubblies in the country.

'Wine is like music,' says Jeff Sinnott, drawing on an analogy close to his heart. 'Back in the 1980s when I was living in Australia, New Zealand bands would come across and describe themselves as "really highly regarded in New Zealand". The fact was internationally they just couldn't foot it. But our pinot noir can.'

When Sinnott moved from Marlborough to Central in 2002, he said that none of the grapes grown at the home vineyard of Amisfield Winery on the shores of Lake Hayes (where he works) could produce table wine. Gibbston Valley and Lake Hayes are good areas for grow-ing grapes to make sparkling wines, says Sinnott, but nothing else.

'The grapes at the lake vineyard take forever to ripen and even if we wanted to make table wine from them, the high fertility levels in the soils means the vines are out of balance so it just doesn't work.'

Consequently, none of Amisfield's grapes for its table wines are grown immediately around the winery.

To find the Amisfield pinot noir vineyards, which make up about 60 percent of production, plus its riesling, sauvignon blanc and pinot gris grapes, you need to drive into the Cromwell Basin – where most of the region's grapes are planted today.

The topography and climate vary widely in the Cromwell Basin but its climate is generally warmer and its soils not as fertile as most places where grapes are grown in the greater Central Otago region. Although most of the vineyards are five years old or less, new clones of pinot noir are predominant rather than the old 10/5 clone that used to form the backbone of pinot noir making in New Zealand.

Location was even more pertinent in 1997 than it is now.

Back then, the Felton Road winery, now internationally renowned for its pinot noir, was just beginning to be established. It is situated at the end of a quiet road, just past the now well-established

ABOVE: Surface schist is everywhere in Central Otago, giving way sometimes to light sandy soils and some clay loams.
RIGHT: Most of the vineyards in the Cromwell Basin are relatively young and large, like this sloping hillside one at Lowburn. Pinot noir is predominant in these vineyards.

Mt Difficulty winery (named after a prominent nearby mountain peak), which is also turning out some of the region's best tasting and most consistent pinot noirs and rieslings. Both of these Bannockburn wineries were thought of as the wild cards in the pack, when they first set up in this area but now, not even a decade later, all of the best tasting pinot noirs from Central are made with grapes planted around Bannockburn, Bendigo, Lowburn, Northburn and all the other areas within and near the Cromwell Basin.

It had become clear, says Blair Walter of Felton Road, that grapes grown in this general area produced more consistent and ripe tasting wines than had been found in previous wines made in other areas of Central Otago.

Now that winemakers have broadly resolved issues of location, in terms of climate, Walter predicts soils and how the land faces the sun will be the deciding factors for new vineyards.

'We will start to see a far greater focus on which side of the hill and which particular patch of that vineyard we should and shouldn't plant different grape varieties on. Some winemakers are already doing that. It's the next key focus for us here.'

Now that the Felton Road home vineyard is 11 years old, Walter wants to convert to herbicide-free practices.

'We're not looking for any certification or big organic stamp on our bottle. We want to be organic because that way we can look after the health of the soil. Increasing the microbiological life of the soil should interact with the vine to give us better expression of the grape variety in each of our wines.'

The Cromwell Basin is so admired by winemakers in the region that Grant Taylor from Gibbston Valley Wines is even planting syrah there.

'In 2000 we made syrah from Gibbston grapes and although they were not totally ripe, the wine was still drinkable,' he says.

'In Cromwell I think we could get some extremely exciting syrahs, so we're putting in a hectare or two and doing it as a trial.'

According to Taylor a hot year like 2002 yields pinot noir grapes from Bendigo in the Cromwell Basin that start to taste port-like.

'You sometimes even begin to wonder if you are actually drinking pinot,' he says, with a bit of a laugh.

'The wines we make from there taste bigger, richer and jammier with flavours of blueberry and licorice rather than the dried herb thing that used to characterise Central Otago pinot noir.'

In a cool year, Taylor describes grapes grown at Gibbston Valley Wines' home vineyard in the Kawarau Gorge as having flavours that verge on green. Though most of the winery's grapes are now coming from warmer vineyards further afield, he says the Gibbston taste has changed noticeably, due to better quality grape clones of pinot noir and lower cropping levels.

'The biggest changes in Central Otago wine come down to what is happening in the vineyard,' explains Taylor. 'This is a region where we need to expose the grapes to the sun, so we are more rigorous about our leaf-plucking and it is giving us more perfumed tasting grapes as a result.'

Greg Hay agrees. He came to Central Otago in 1987 to help his brother, Rob Hay, establish Chard Farm. For the first three years, they put in vineyard posts, plants and irrigation, and did everything else that needed to be done. Then, when the grapes started coming, Greg looked after the vines while Rob made the wine. They parted ways

in the 1990s in order to pursue their own ventures. Rob still owns Chard Farm and is a part owner at Amisfield and Greg has established Peregrine Wines. And, going back to that old location debate, Greg Hay says that, in a hot year, 'Gibbston Valley grapes are fantastic'.

'Gibbston's climate gives the grapes the ability to sit out there for four to six weeks longer than the fruit from the other side [Cromwell Basin] and truly develop really silky wines of elegance rather than blockbuster big fruit bombs.'

Not that there is anything wrong with blockbuster pinot noirs from Central Otago. The fact is, the best Central Otago pinot noirs – big and fruity or not – possess what many wine fanatics describe as more elegance than most other New Zealand pinot noirs.

'Gibbston can only be described as a marginal viticultural region,' says Grant Taylor, winemaker at Gibbston Valley Wines.

Both he and Hay – and most other winemakers in the region – concede that, even with rigorous attention to grape clonal selection, lots of pruning and extreme leaf-plucking, Gibbston Valley-grown grapes demand attention levels that exceed financial gain, much of the time.

As Hay says, grapes grown in Lowburn and other sites in the Cromwell Basin are like money in the bank – in any given year.

The biggest challenge in Cromwell Basin, says Hay, is that in a hot year winemakers need to be careful that their grapes don't get too sugar ripe before they are physiologically ripe.

'In Cromwell, you don't need to be as vigorous with leaf-plucking. You actually want to stop too much sun from getting on the fruit, to slow the hot year vintage conditions down.'

The flipside is that in a cool year in Gibbston winemakers will be grateful to have some grapes grown in that warmer region.

'The reason we grow grapes on both sides is to show that pinot noir is a textural wine. That doesn't come from only one component grown in one climate.'

Hay's biggest aim is to produce pinot noir that people can afford to buy. As new grapevines start producing fruit (in winemaker lingo they 'come on-stream'), he says that he plans to then produce a declassified pinot noir.

'Young vines don't impart much to a top quality wine but they can contribute to a decent tasting pinot noir without the complexity of a top wine but also without the big price tag,' explains Hay.

'What we're trying to achieve with Peregrine is the best value for money pinot noir we can possibly make.

'Winemaking in Central has gone from being like a cottage garden industry to being a commercial business where the spectrum of skills required has changed dramatically. Now you need dedicated marketing, winemakers and distributors. In the past we were jacks of all trades.' Greg Hay, Peregrine Wines

Tourism is huge business in Central Otago, due to the sheer beauty of the landscape, its sprawling unpopulated holiday spots, large number of beautiful lakes and a never-ending stream of outdoor activities from bungy jumping to white water rafting, snow skiing, kayaking and paragliding … the list keeps growing, as outdoorsy types keep reinventing thrill sports. The growth in the region's tourism industry translates directly to the growth in its wine scene.

Not only do tourists want to drink wine from Central Otago, many of them want to have a part in owning it.

For a long time, a two hectare block of grapes was an average size in the region. Now, the average size of a vineyard is between 10 and 15 hectares, says Greg Hay.

FAR LEFT: Winemaker and owner Rob Hay of Chard Farm winery was one of the region's earliest modern wine pioneers, planting his first vines in 1987 with his brother Greg Hay.
LEFT: Chard Farm sits evocatively on a sunny site in the Kawarau Gorge, which links the tourist town of Queenstown on the shores of Lake Wakatipu with the vineyards in the Cromwell Basin.
ABOVE: Central Otago winemaker Duncan Forsyth and his daughter Alex, standing outside Peregrine Wines.

When the Hay brothers planted Chard Farm, it doubled Central Otago's wine industry with an initial eight hectare block. Up until 1995 there was, Hay says, 'virtually nothing going on here'.

In fact, from 1994 to 1995, the land planted in grapes dropped two hectares from 48 to 46 hectares. After that the region's vineyard growth exploded. Suddenly people started realising that Central Otago could produce some solid quality driven pinot noirs rather than just gimmicky southern wines.

Fast growth has also occurred this millennium in Central because several grape-growers joined forces. This is how both Peregrine and Mt Difficulty and several other wineries in the region managed to begin business by making quantities of wine that, while not huge, are big enough to be distributed widely in New Zealand and maintain a strong presence in the restaurants within the region itself.

When Hay established Peregrine Wines in the late 1990s, he searched for land throughout Central Otago and found 130 hectares planted on 12 to 14 vineyards, all spread out in different areas. Many of the vineyards are owned by shareholders in Peregrine, freeing up other available capital for building a new winery production facility and large tasting area, which opened for the 2004 vintage.

'It works well because they own the land, we manage the blocks uniformly to achieve quality production rather than quantity, and we pay them accordingly.

'We can afford to do things to the vineyards this way that we might not be able to otherwise: cutting off shoulder bunches, crop thinning, going to the "nth degree" to make sure that what comes out the other end is the best possible fruit.'

Vineyard expansion will slow down in the region, insists Hay, adding that this is a necessary breather, which will allow wineries to sort out infrastructure issues.

Within the next half decade, one of the biggest challenges in the region will be the lack of winery production facilities.

'Huge demand will be placed on existing wineries because there is a shortage of production facilities here, as well as a shortage of workers and a shortage of housing for those workers because of the skyrocketing property prices.'

He predicts that small wineries making good quality wine will be able to rely on mail order and gate sales, while larger wineries will remain viable because of the economies of scale.

'But I have an inkling that there will be an unhappy middle ground in there for those who have not done their marketing and distribution homework. It's easy to overlook those pragmatic details when you're busy planting pinot noir.'

LEFT: It's rare to see Lake Hayes looking anything other than mirror-like and flat.
ABOVE: A small cluster of historic stone buildings blends into the dry countryside at Peregrine Wines, Central Otago.

When Amisfield winemaker Jeff Sinnott arrived in the region, he cautioned the winery owners, Rob Hay, John Darby and Tom Tusher, not to plant any more vineyards. Yet.

The winery has 40 hectares of grapes in the ground and another 60 hectares ready to be planted. But Sinnott insists that the best thing to do now is to wait and see if the market is there for the wine that will flow out of Central Otago by the middle of the decade, before increasing production further.

Like Peregrine, and others, Amisfield's vineyard is divided into several distinctive blocks of land, each owned by different partners in the business as well as by friends who are contract grape-growers. All of the vineyards are managed by the winery to the same exacting standards and the growers are getting a premium price for their grapes without being involved in growing them in a hands-on way.

Talk about white wines to Central Otago winemakers and there are three reactions. The most common one is the distracted winemaker who turns the conversation back to pinot noir. Then there is the chardonnay fan, devoted to making the white queen of the wine world in this cool region. And then there are the winemakers who realise that both riesling and pinot gris from this region can taste sensational. For reasons no one has quite yet fathomed, these latter two aromatic white grapes express themselves with incredible clarity when made from the grapes that are grown in this often marginal winemaking region.

Felton Road winemaker Blair Walter has a foot in each of the last two camps. He makes one of New Zealand's best rieslings, yet this grape only constitutes about 10 percent of the winery's vineyard area and there are no plans to increase it. On the other hand, Walter has about 15 percent of the total Felton Road vineyard planted in chardonnay grapes and he is passionate about making a top-shelf chardonnay from the region.

'We had a little bit of pinot blanc planted but I've got permission to pull the chainsaw out to get rid of it and put in more chardonnay in its place. And given how well chardonnay does next to pinot noir in Burgundy, we ought to be focusing on it here,' explains Walter.

This could make sense, given that the Felton Road vineyards are in the region's warmest areas. Other winemakers continue to make chardonnay, due to the high demand in the world for this wine.

'It takes a lot of work to make chardonnay from Central grapes,' says Grant Taylor from Gibbston Valley winery.

In order to rise to that challenge, Taylor is changing the way he makes chardonnay. He is sourcing most chardonnay grapes from

ABOVE: An old car passes new vineyards, which are everywhere in the Cromwell Basin, as here at Bendigo Station.
RIGHT: Arrowtown, nestled into the hills, is still a bustling little centre today. One of the few remaining historic gold towns in the region, it is filled with relics of that long-gone rush era in the late 1800s.

warmer regions within the Cromwell Basin rather than in Gibbston Valley. He is also refining winemaking techniques, stirring the lees (dead yeast cells, which impart flavour and texture to wine) every four or five days to build texture in chardonnay.

'There's a lot of bad chardonnay out there and you stop drinking it because it's just not interesting. I want to drink a chardonnay once in a while and try to make something that I enjoy and that other drinkers will say "wow" to.'

Riesling is generally better suited to the region than chardonnay, Taylor believes.

'That's pretty obvious when you taste the riesling from here but it's not a strong focus for many people,' he says, adding quietly that if he could, he would focus strongly on this aromatic white grape.

Riesling has not been given much consideration in Central because the focus has been so strongly on pinot noir.

'I think we can make great riesling down here but with riesling, as with other grapes, vine age is hugely important to get depth of flavour. Since most people do not focus on riesling we have a long way to go to see the best that can come from here.'

Felton Road's riesling more than hints at greatness, but not much is made. Mt Difficulty winemaker Matt Dicey is fashioning rieslings in the mould of Mosel's most delicately styled wines. This harking back to the old world of wine seems crazily inappropriate, as it reinforces the wine jargon that many wine lovers try to avoid, but it is the best way to describe Dicey's deliciously intense, light styled riesling.

Dicey describes himself as a riesling fanatic and is only sorry that the general populace does not always feel the same way.

'I would love to make more riesling because even in the short time we have had down here to try it out, all of the signs show that the climate and conditions here can make a riesling that is unique in New Zealand and has the ability to age extremely well, developing and improving in the bottle in at least the short and medium term.

'Once our grapevines are older we could probably start to make riesling for the very long haul, for those who like aged styles and want to keep it, but that will be years away.'

It will also take a quantum shift in the national palate to give Dicey and others like him the impetus to make more riesling for a country where the favourite wines are sauvignon blanc and chardonnay.

Which brings us to pinot gris. Nationwide plantings of this grape variety have grown from just 22 hectares of land in 1995 to nearly 400 hectares in 2005. Central's share in all this is tiny, but the quality is extremely high.

Amisfield's Jeff Sinnott is putting enormous energy into making pinot gris in a style that is immediately appealing, even when it is still fermenting. A taste of the cloudy, still-fermenting grape juice is like drinking freshly squeezed guavas. And that is only one component of the wine-to-be. It can also be soft, round and textural.

'I am working hard to harness the most complex and enjoyable flavours from this grape,' he says.

Dicey at Mt Difficulty makes a multi-faceted expression of pinot gris that generally has yet to find its feet in the sense of what style it can be when grown in New Zealand.

Sinnott's folly, he says, is a half hectare block of riesling grapes grown in the Cromwell Basin at the extensive, rolling, flat and variable Amisfield Vineyard.

This particular little slice of land is perfectly suited to riesling, says Sinnott, who hopes to make an ice wine from the grapes some years and a top quality riesling or two the rest of the time.

He is passionate about all of the aromatic white grapes growing on the Amisfield vineyards, describing sauvignon blanc grapes grown at Lowburn as tasting eerily like Marlborough sauvignon blanc.

'The wine we make from it has palate weight and vinosity and texture that I haven't seen out of Central Otago sauvignon. I would not want to make a lot of it but it's very exciting stuff.'

Master of Wine Steve Smith, a minor shareholder in Peregrine Wines and a viticulturist, says: 'My whole view on making riesling for New Zealand is to make it in very small quantities and to make it very good.'

One of the best wine styles from Central is bubbly. Winemaker Rudi Bauer of Quartz Reef produces a champagne-like sparkling wine from grapes grown at the north-east end of Lake Dunstan, by Bendigo Station in the Cromwell Basin.

Jeff Sinnott also makes very good bubbly from grapes grown on the cool shores of Lake Hayes. A smattering of other very high quality bubblies has been produced in Central.

Central Otago bubbly has an inimitable crispness and freshness that distinguishes it from other New Zealand sparkling wine and gives it far more credibility with champagne drinkers and lovers of good bubblies made in this country to date. Although quantities are minute these bubblies deserve to be taken seriously. Watch this space.

ABOVE: Lake Hayes Vineyard winemaker Jeff Sinnott (left) at the new Amisfield winery, 20 minutes' drive from Queenstown.
RIGHT: Chardonnay and pinot noir vines are grown solely to turn into sparking wines on the shores on Lake Hayes at Amisfield's vineyards.

Central Otago wineries

Alexandra Wine Company

75 Rockview Road, Alexandra, Central Otago, phone (03) 448 8573

Amisfield Vineyards/Lake Hayes Winery

10 Lake Hayes Road, Lake Hayes, Arrowtown, phone (03) 442 0556

Black Ridge Winery

Conroy's Road, Alexandra, Central Otago, phone (03) 449 2059

Carrick Winery

Cairnmuir Road, Bannockburn, Cromwell, Central Otago,

phone (03) 445 3480

Chard Farm Vineyard

Chard Road, Gibbston, Central Otago, phone (03) 442 6110

Felton Road Wines

319 Felton Road, Bannockburn, Central Otago, phone (03) 445 0881

Gibbston Valley Wines

Queenstown-Cromwell Highway, Gibbston, Central Otago,

phone (03) 442 6910

Kawarau Estate

Cromwell-Wanaka Highway, Lowburn, Central Otago,

phone (03) 215 9311

Lake Hayes and Amisfield Vineyards

Cnr Lake Hayes Road and State Highway 6, Lake Hayes, Central Otago,

phone (03) 442 0556

Leaning Rock Vineyard

188 Hillview Road, Alexandra, Central Otago, phone (03) 448 9169

Mt Difficulty Wines

Felton Road, Bannockburn, Central Otago, phone (03) 445 3445

Mount Edward Winery

34 Coalpit Road, Gibbston Valley, Central Otago, phone (03) 442 6113

Mount Maude Winery

Maungawera Valley Road, Wanaka, Central Otago,

phone (03) 443 8398

Mount Michael Vineyard

McNab Road, Cromwell, Central Otago, phone (03) 445 1351

Olssen's of Bannockburn

306 Felton Road, Bannockburn, Central Otago, phone (03) 445 1716

Peregrine Wines Central Otago

Kawarau Gorge Road, Gibbston, Central Otago, phone (03) 442 4000

Quartz Reef

c/- PO Box 63, Cromwell, Central Otago, phone (03) 445 3084

Rippon Vineyard

Mt Aspiring Road, Rapid No 246, Lake Wanaka, Central Otago,

phone (03) 443 8084

Taramea Wines

Speargrass Flat Road, RD1, Queenstown, phone (03) 442 1453

Two Paddocks

c/- Box 722, Queenstown, phone (03) 442 5988

Waitiri Creek Wines

Church Lane, Gibbston Valley, Central Otago, phone (03) 441 3315

William Hill Vineyard

Dunstan Road, Alexandra, Central Otago, phone (03) 448 8436

Special thanks

Bibliography

Special thanks go to the following people; if I have left anybody off the list, it is entirely my fault and I apologise unreservedly. Enormous thanks from me and photographer Andrew Coffey to: Allan Scott of Allan Scott Wines; Avis New Zealand and Rachael O'Connor; Babich Wines, David, Joe and Peter Babich; Browns Boutique Hotel in Queenstown; Destination Queenstown; Cathedral Inn, Nelson; Church Road Winery and Tony Prichard in Hawke's Bay; Collard Brothers Wines and the late Lionel Collard in Auckland; Craggy Range winery, Steve Smith and Doug Wisor in Hawke's Bay; Daniel Schuster Fine Wines and Danny and Mari Schuster in Waipara; Escarpment Vineyard and Larry McKenna in Martinborough; Esk Valley Estate, Gordon Russell and team; Gina Hochstein, designer; Hawke's Bay Promotions, Harvest Hawke's Bay and Hawke's Bay Vintners; Jan Gardner for her research and organisational work; Kowhai Cottage in Nelson; Marianne (aka Chic) and Neil Mackie from Glencarrigh Homestay in Gisborne; Montana Wines, Zirk van den Berg, Jeff Clarke and Gerry Gregg; Mount Riley Wines, John Buchanan and Sheryle Linthwaite; Mountford Estate and Buffy and Michael Eaton in Waipara; Muddy Water Fine Wines, Belinda Gould and Jane East in Waipara; Neudorf Vineyard and Judy and Tim Finn; Palliser Estate Wines and Richard Riddiford in Martinborough; Peregrine Wines, Duncan Forsyth and Greg Hay in Central Otago; The Old Manse in Martinborough and John Hargrave; Trinity Hill Winery and John Hancock in Hawke's Bay; Villa Maria Wines and George Fistonich and Ian Clark; Winegrowers New Zealand and chief executive officer, Philip Gregan.

Cooper, Michael, *The Wines and Vineyards of New Zealand*, fifth ed., Hodder Moa Beckett, 1996

Cooper, Michael, *Wine Atlas of New Zealand*, Hodder Moa Beckett, 2002

Forrestal, Peter (ed.), *The Global Encyclopedia of Wine*, Harper Collins, 2000

Robinson, Jancis (ed.), *The Oxford Companion to Wine*, Oxford University Press, 1994

Robinson, Jancis, *Guide to Wine Grapes*, Oxford University Press, 1996

Scott, Dick and Marti Friedlander, *Pioneers of New Zealand Wine*, second ed., Reed Publishing NZ Ltd, 2002

Feedback on this book can be given to the author via email: jthomson@xtra.co.nz